CW00666633

THE LOST ART OF PUTTING

Introducing the Six Putting Performance Principles

By Gary Nicol and Karl Morris

With a foreword from the 1999 Open champion Paul Lawrie

About Sports Publications

Sports Publications are specialist golf publishers across magazines, books and digital formats.

Sports Publications are the publishers of National Club Golfer, Lady Golfer, Go Golfing, Society Guide, Pro Trade +, The Golf Club Manager, Great Golf in England and BIGGA's Your Course as well as **nationalclubgolfer.com, lady-golfer.com** and several external titles.

The Lost Art of Putting was edited by Dan Murphy, editorial director at Sports Publications.

Published in 2018 in Great Britain. All rights reserved.
Published by Sports Publications Limited,
2 Arena Park, Leeds, LS17 9BF.
www.sports-publications.com
@SPPublications

ISBN: 978-1-5272-2585-5

CONTENTS

4   **Foreword** By Paul Lawrie

6   **Introduction**

16   **Chapter 1:** What is your story?

27   **Expert Insight:** Trackman and putting

36   **Chapter 2:** Attention

51   **Expert Insight:** The Yips

58   **Chapter 3:** Two Questions

68   **Expert Insight:** Putting data

74   **Chapter 4:** Line and pace

96   **Expert Insight:** Putter design

104   **Chapter 5:** Green reading

118   **Expert Insight:** Greenkeeping

122   **Chapter 6:** Visualisation

134   **Expert Insight:** Visualisation

140   **Conclusion**

FOREWORD
by Paul Lawrie, 1999 Open champion

FROM the day I turned professional in 1986, I am proud to say I have always been prepared to work on my game in order to improve. As a young professional, I always believed that a good work ethic and the desire to succeed would bring rewards. That belief and desire, along with my love for the game of golf, is still as strong as it ever was.

Working hard is one thing but working on the right things is undoubtedly more important.

One part of my game which has at times been a great source of pride, as well as occasional frustration, is my putting. To become a happy, fulfilled and successful golfer, I firmly believe that the ability to hole putts when it really matters is what separates the best from the rest.

When I have won tournaments around the world and while playing my part on Ryder Cup teams, yes, I have hit great shots, and yes, my short game has been in good shape – but ultimately that counts for nothing if you can't hole putts.

Splitting fairways with perfectly struck drives and flushing iron shots to within a few feet of the hole is enormously satisfying but nothing compares to holing that winning putt.

The feelings I experienced when lifting the famous Claret Jug after winning the Open Championship at Carnoustie in 1999 were largely down to my ability to hole putts when I needed to that week.

The memories of which are still as vivid today as they were on that incredible Sunday afternoon.

I have never underestimated the importance of being a good putter and the enjoyment that can bring to golfers of all standards.

I now realise that, when putting my best, I was actually using a lot of the tools and techniques you are about to read on the pages of this book. Gary and Karl have distilled what can be made an overly complicated and confusing subject into simple, practical and, above all, effective principles.

If you embrace them they will have a big impact on your game.

In 2001 we set up the Paul Lawrie Foundation to ensure that golf was accessible to every young person across Aberdeen and Aberdeenshire and with the hope that one day we might help to produce a major champion. Since then, the Foundation has gone from strength to strength and recently I have begun to play golf more often with the kids and young adults coming through our Foundation programmes.

We focus a lot on course and game management; much more so than on technical aspects. I continually preach the importance of working more on short-game (and specifically putting) than on any other area of the game. Again, many of the principles we discuss during these rounds are the same as you'll find within the pages of this book. Golf has given me so much and for that I shall be forever grateful. My journey has been fantastic and I wish you well in your own personal quest to become the best possible golfer and putter you can be with the aid of this insightful and helpful book.

All the very best,
Paul Lawrie

• Paul is a two-time Ryder Cup player, eight-time winner on the European Tour, and the Open champion at Carnoustie in 1999. Learn more about Paul and his foundation at **paullawriegolf.com**, **paullawriefoundation.co.uk** and **paullawriegolfcentre.co.uk**

AN INTRODUCTION
from the authors

WE will start not by telling you anything but by asking you a simple question: Why are you here?

Just pause for a moment and think about this particular question.

Of all the things you could be doing in your life you are sitting reading a book on putting. We thank you for that!

By the very nature of asking questions, as you will discover later in the book, you have probably already come up with some form of answer to this line of enquiry.

Your brain will have instantly 'gone to work' on the reasons why you bought this book.

You will have encountered a personal experience of how questions hold your attention while you search for an answer. Questions are weapons you will be able to use in the battle to have your attention in the places you want it to be to serve you the best in your quest to hole more putts.

This simple but profound point will be a cornerstone of what you are about to read.

As the 2010 US Open champion Graeme McDowell once said to us: "Questions are indeed the answer!"

One such question which really got us thinking is: "Does the putt create the stroke or does the stroke create the putt?"

We have asked this question many times and the resultant answers heavily influenced the content of the following pages. Take a moment to think about this question, and indeed this concept, as it is vitally important if you are to remove your current putting shackles and enable you to embark on an amazing journey with us.

But more on questions later in the book. We will now make something of an assumption.

Our guess is that in some way you find yourself reading this as a result of your past experiences on the greens being something less than you either wanted or expected.

You haven't yet become the putter you wish to be.

It may be something of an arrogant assumption on our part, but we are assuming you find yourself here not as a result of being a great putter but as a result of being something less than you know you potentially can be. If you are not in that category and you are already great on the greens then we apologise – but please stay with us anyway!

It is with this idea in mind that we want to share with you what we hope is a different perspective.

Note we didn't say the correct perspective. Golf is full of interpretation and opinion and if the way you currently interpret the best way to roll the ball into the hole is working for you, then the most important thing is you continue to do exactly that.

If there is one single truth the two of us have discovered in the best part of 60 years' combined coaching experience, it is that the game of golf is not about finding 'the' way to do it but more a case of discovering, or perhaps more importantly uncovering, 'your' way to do it.

However, the perspective and concepts we want to share with you are ones we know have the potential to liberate you – not just on the greens but in the whole of your golf game and, as much as it may seem a push, the rest of your life.

It is our firm belief you can create a cascade of golfing improvement by having some personal breakthrough on the greens through your understanding and application of our Putting Performance Principles.

The way you are in one part of the game will often be reflected in other parts. The perspective we want to share with you is not a 'do this my way' or 'do it because x tour pro does it' type of coaching but rather a set of ideas you will need to personalise for yourself. Putting strokes and styles are like fingerprints – they are unique and our own.

"Golf can be a difficult game but it's a little easier if you trust your instincts," said Nancy Lopez, the winner of 48 LPGA tournaments, including three majors. "It's too hard a game to try and play like someone else."

In personalising the information for yourself, you will get to own for yourself the information. This will be you taking action and responsibility as opposed to just blindly following someone else's opinion.

It is our conviction that putting is being taught in a way that is holding many people back. Not everybody, but a lot of people. Our assumption is that you may be one of them.

It is curious that such a simple action as moving an implement a few feet away from your hands can cause so many problems. It is nothing short of amazing for most golfers that the best days they had on the greens were back in the mists of time, perhaps in their junior golfing days. So much for the idea of experience being vital!

Why is it the vast majority of people tend to become worse at an activity that has little to no physical demands in the way hitting a booming tee shot obviously has?

Anyone who has played this great game will know that golf is very much played between the ears.

However, the golf coaching world would have us believe that the way forward is to make physical changes and "improvements".

We beg to differ.

Having had the pleasure of working with thousands of golfers of all standards, from beginners to the winners of major championships, experience has shown us that the biggest and most lasting improvements are made through adopting some different concepts to your approach, rather than trying to master or perfect physical skills or movements.

Paradoxically you may be very surprised to find how your physical motion improves as a result of a different concept of what you are actually trying to do.

Some of the game's greatest players have been driven to distraction by the simple act of rolling a ball towards a target.

Famously, the great Ben Hogan believed putting should be made a lesser part of the game, so much did the putting demons consume him.

Over the years we have both seen a number of careers cut short with troubles on the greens. We see no need for this as we will deal with later on in the book. What you believe deep down about your putting will manifest itself into a self-imposed reality. You become the story you tell yourself the most often.

This book will help you to shape a new story: to begin afresh if you like, to construct the story you want that is useful to you as opposed to a story imposed upon you by your automatic patterns and habits.

A breakthrough in one area of your game can extend the sense of what is possible in your golfing future.

There may well be people who read this book who make their living from the game of golf and to those we extend a warm welcome but this book is not just about the better player: it is about the game of golf and those who play it in all their shapes, sizes and abilities.

Golf is good for you physically, mentally, emotionally and – dare we say it – spiritually if you have an approach to the game that allows you to get the benefits the game has to offer you.

If you have an attitude that is keeping you 'one shot from insanity' or 'one missed putt from hell' then you will have a tough relationship with the game and it will in the end beat you up.

We want you to look at your golfing future through the lens of what is possible. If, through rolling the ball better on the greens, you get some insights into what you are truly capable of, then we have done our job. We hope to liberate you from what we see is an overly scientific view of the game and connect you back to the art of putting.

We are not in any way diminishing science and we will ask for the assistance of science in parts of the book to help us explain our perspective and concepts, but it is in the lost art of putting and the freedom to express what is a more natural way to roll the ball into the hole we know will set you free to putt in a more child-like way.

We are aiming to help you become more childlike on the greens and less childish.

There is a big difference between the two – we see far too much of the latter and nowhere near enough of the former especially on the various world tours.

To be childlike is to have a simple fascination in getting the ball into the hole and to love the task of doing so. To be childish is to expect a certain outcome will come your way, that you 'deserve' to hole the putt or that you shouldn't miss from a certain distance.

As we will discover, one of the things you can never own is the outcome of a putt and if getting upset about an outcome was a prerequisite for holing more putts in the future then this book would never have needed to be written.

We will shortly introduce you to what we call the Putting Performance Principles – a set of ideas you can take and personalise in your own unique way and style.

You will, perhaps for the first time, 'own' your own putting stroke. We like to say that you have 'found your way home'. More importantly you will then be able to direct your attention to getting the ball into the hole on a more regular basis.

From our perspective we see so many golfers getting worse and worse on the greens as a result of what they are currently putting their attention on.

Any natural ability we have to judge both distance and direction can be severely hampered if we make the whole exercise like a mathematical equation.

We demonstrate this in our putting workshops when we simply throw a ball to a player and then ask them to throw it back. As they are doing this we will start to move further away and then nearer to them. Almost every time the player will find our hand in an unerringly accurate way. Time after time they judge both the distance and the direction with incredible accuracy.

Yet when we ask them how far they need to take their arm back and through on the next try their performance starts to drop.

We get in our own way by being overly conscious of what is a natural skill. We also see so many players obsessing their attention at the putter end of things as opposed to the hole end of things.

Rather than obsessing about the start line, why not pay attention to the finishing line? From trying to make the 'perfect' stroke (whatever that is) to trying to get the perfect start line or aiming to roll the ball along a chalk line.

All of these things we will explain, as we spend our time together, are getting in the way of what we hope you are trying to do, which is actually get the golf ball to fall into the hole.

So often in an attempt to make scientifically pure or perfect strokes, we lose sight of the fact that we are actually trying to get a golf ball to have a simple relationship with a hole in the ground, momentum and gravity.

If we are able to better judge the pace of a putt, we allow gravity to do its job and the gravitational force will overcome momentum. That little white ball will find its way more often into what we will explain as actually being a bigger hole if you get your pace correct on a more regular basis. In essence, you are about to discover the lost art of putting.

Much of what we will discuss will require you to have an open mind. Perhaps you will have to suspend some of the beliefs you have carried around with you for a while as to the best way of holing putts.

Our premise is that if you have tested a belief for a number of years and it hasn't produce the results you want, then another couple of years acting on the same beliefs will unfortunately only produce more of the same results.

It's Einstein's cliché: "The definition of insanity is to keep doing the same things over and over again and expect a different result."

We hope our approach will provide something of a breath of fresh air for you as you get excited about the possibility of being great on the greens. Just imagine what this could mean for your game in the future. We want you to become genuinely excited about discovering something which has always been there but has just been in the captivity of over analysis for far too long.

We want you to begin to conceive of a future time when you are excited to walk on to a green with a sense of what you could do as opposed to being concerned about what might go wrong. To fall in love with the idea of creating this putt in this unique moment.

Nothing in what we suggest will mean you are guaranteed to hole every putt but we do believe you can create a set of conditions to give yourself one heck of a chance.

We will also help you to create a mindset whereby the outcome of the putt may not be under your control but the way you react to that outcome most definitely will be.

So many of our reactions to events we don't like are habitual but perhaps what we don't realise is these very reactions can be embedding the roots of future failure.

We want you to become in control of your reactions as opposed to being a passive victim of an automatic habit that may well have been holding you back for years.

It is our conviction that no matter how long you have been playing this great game, it is never too late to learn and master skills such as intention and attention.

We feel these skills are needed more than ever in a modern world doing everything it possibly can to destroy our ability to pay attention for even a moment to what we are actually doing.

The devices we all carry around with us all day, our phones, can do some wonderful things but it is our contention that it can be deadly in terms of your attention. We are training our brain to 'flicker' in terms of attention. As you keep looking at your phone you flit from one thing to another without really becoming absorbed in anything. Does this make you happy? Probably not.

Your brain is at its very best when it is present and focused on what is right in front of you now as opposed to being in a constant state of low- level distraction.

Putting could even be a laboratory to help you to train your mind in other areas of your life in which you want to excel, be that your business or your personal relationships. To develop the skill of focused attention is exceptionally useful in all areas of your life where you wish to excel and reveal more of your true capability.

We firmly believe the quality of your life will be directly related to your ability to have your attention in a place you want it to be as opposed to where society tries to take you to suit its own agenda.

We are hoping, above all else, to have some fun with this.

Both of us get an immense amount of pleasure from seeing the faces of our students light up as they experience what can actually be achieved on the greens.

It is a pleasure to see such a release and a breakthrough as simplicity sets free a motion that has been drugged into numbness by complexity. Over the years in the putting schools we run, we have both experienced some genuine breakthroughs and light-bulb moments as our students see and welcome a new perspective.

This is our goal in our time together: to adjust or even change your perspective as opposed to trying to change your stroke as everyone else does.

What we will add is that, if your perspective changes, it is very interesting to see what happens to your stroke as a by-product or consequence of that shift in perspective.

On the other hand, if your perspective stays the same no amount of work on your putting stoke will really make much difference.

Let's start our journey of discovery together,

Gary and Karl

Key takeaways

1 If you change your perspective and concepts around putting this will have the potential to liberate you on the greens to experience what you are truly capable of.

2 The biggest and most lasting golfing improvements are made through adopting and applying a different mental outlook and approach, rather than trying to master or perfect physical skills or movements.
Paradoxically when concepts change physical movement often improves.

3 What you believe deep down about your putting will manifest itself into a self-imposed reality. You become the story you tell yourself the most often. This book will help you to shape a new story and to begin afresh.

4 If we are able to better judge the pace of a putt, that little white ball will find its way more often into what we will explain as actually being a bigger hole.

5 Imagine being excited to walk on to a green with a sense of what you could do as opposed to being concerned about what might go wrong.

Chapter 1
WHAT IS YOUR STORY?

MANY years ago, we heard a story about the legendary coach Harvey Penick, author of the international best-seller the Little Red Golf Book.

Penick was the golf coach at the University of Texas from 1931 to 1963, coaching the team to 21 championships in 33 years, including 20 out of 23 seasons from 1932 to 1954.

He coached Hall of Fame members such as Tom Kite, Ben Crenshaw, Mickey Wright and Kathy Whitworth. Many people consider him to be one of the greatest golf coaches who ever lived.

The tale concerns a dinner he had with Kite and Crenshaw just before they were both about to embark on their professional careers. Kite asked the wise old coach if there was one single piece of advice he would offer to help them in their career.

Penick considered the question for a moment then said: "Make sure you go to dinner with good putters."

In what can easily be perceived as a trite or flippant statement lie the words of a genius.

What Penick knew instinctively was that good putters talk about the putts they hole. They believe they are going to hole putts while poor putters indulge in a 'pity party' of all the putts they have missed.

These stories become our reality. If we tell ourselves a story enough times we actually become the story.

We also remember the story in a Bob Rotella book about perhaps the greatest pressure putter of all time, Jack Nicklaus.

During a presentation to an audience at his son's university, the all-time leading major winner said: "I have never missed from inside three feet on the back nine of a major tournament on Sunday."

Sitting in the audience was a man either brave enough or stupid enough to challenge the Golden Bear.

"But Mr Nicklaus," he said. "I saw you recently in the US Senior Open and you definitely missed one from inside three feet on the back nine."

The audience went quiet and Nicklaus looked at the man.

With as much grace as he could muster, he glared and said: "I have never missed from inside three feet on the back nine of a major."

Attempting to move on, he started to talk again.

"But Mr Nicklaus," pleaded the man, "I have it on video. I can send it to you if you like."

But Jack was having none of it. He maintained he had never missed from inside three feet on the back nine of a major.

That was his story and he was sticking to it.

Has Jack Nicklaus ever missed from inside three feet on the back nine of a major? Of course he has. Does he choose to tell himself that story?

Of course not. The great man is either deluding himself or he is choosing a story that is useful to him.

As human beings we are basically just a walking, talking book of stories. We are a collection of interpretations and assumptions. A missed putt in and of itself means nothing beyond the meaning we personally attach to it. Great putters tend to adopt a good attitude to putting. Your story will determine or at the very least, heavily influence your attitude.

Now, here is the key: the stories you tell yourself will either be useful to you or useless, exactly the same principle we will discover with attention. The narrative will either support your goals and ambitions or the stories will hold you back. What you will produce in the outside world will be relative to the stories you keep telling yourself. The stories we tell ourselves can begin to act out, even at a subconscious level.

The power of changing your narrative

One of the world's most influential psychologists is Dr Ellen Langer. She was the first female tenured psychology professor at Harvard. She shared with us some fascinating research she had done on stories and perception with a group of chambermaids.

Dr Langer is a lifelong researcher who has published several groundbreaking and provocative studies. In this particular study, she decided to look at whether our perception of how much exercise we are getting has any actual effect on how our bodies actually look.

As anybody in the hotel industry knows, hotel chambermaids spend their days moving heavy bedding, linen and equipment around endless hotel corridors and floors as well as polishing and cleaning. Almost every moment of their working lives involves engagement in some kind of physical activity.

But Dr Langer found, unbelievably, that most of these women didn't see themselves as physically active. In a survey, 67 per cent reported that they didn't exercise.

More than a third of those reported said they didn't get any exercise at all! This was the story they told themselves, the narrative they held in their mind, albeit at a subconscious level.

"Given that they are exercising all day long, this seemed totally bizarre," said Dr Langer.

What was even more bizarre was that, despite the fact all of the women in her study far exceeded the US surgeon general's recommendation for daily exercise, the bodies of the women did not seem to benefit from their activity. Their bodies reflected what they believed in terms of the exercise. Many of the chambermaids carried excess weight on their bodies.

Dr Langer and her team measured the maids' body fat, waist-to-hip ratio, blood pressure, weight and body mass index. They found all of these indicators matched the maids' perceived amount of exercise, rather than their actual amount of exercise.

So Dr Langer set about changing their story. She put in place the beginnings of a different narrative. A different explanation of 'reality'.

She divided 84 maids into two groups. With one group, researchers carefully went through each of the tasks they did each day, explaining how many calories those tasks burned. They were informed that the activity already met the definition of an active lifestyle. A new and refreshing story. The other group was given no information at all and they just carried on as normal.

One month later, Dr Langer and her team of researchers returned to take physical measurements of the women and were surprised by what they found. In the group that had been given a different story about the amount of exercise they were doing each day, there was a decrease in their weight, waist-to-hip ratio — and a 10 per cent drop in blood pressure.

One possible explanation is that the process of learning about the amount of exercise they were already getting somehow changed the maids' behaviour.

But Dr Langer says that her team surveyed both the women and their managers and found no indication that the maids had altered their routines in any way. She believes the change can be explained only by the change in the women's mindset. The story they told themselves had been changed and this actually affected their weight and health markers.

For us, this is mind-blowing and the consequences profound.

In many ways, it defies logic but we have seen this time and time again in our coaching careers: the power of the personal story.

Can you begin to see how your own narrative of your putting capability has such a long-term effect on your performance?

More importantly, unless you change your narrative your body will always find a way of missing putts just as the chambermaids 'found' a way of storing excess fat on their body despite moving constantly through the day in a way that should have burned off the excess weight.

What the thinker thinks the prover proves

Trevor Sylvestor, a great therapist, taught us the concept of the Thinker and the Prover: what the thinker thinks the prover proves.

So, if we think we are poor on the greens then the 'prover' inside our minds will seek supporting evidence of that thought.

Every three-putt is a confirmation of the story. Every stroke feeling a bit jerky and every long putt left short is the opportunity for the prover to 'prove' I am a poor putter.

Any evidence to counter that belief is ignored. The putts rolled smoothly, the birdie putts that go in, the great lag putt from 50 feet? They are all passed over because the thinker thinks we are poor at putting so it doesn't in any way go looking for any evidence to contradict that story.

The thinker loves to help the prover by talking about how many putts we have taken. He draws company in the misery of poor putting. He tries to recruit other 'believers' who just love to draw out more and more evidence of the struggle on the greens. There is almost a badge of honour worn by people who putt badly and they are only too willing to share it with others.

In his book the Luck Factor, Professor Richard Wiseman explores the concept of luck. Does it in fact really exist or is it more about the story we tell ourselves about how lucky we are and how that story will influence our perception of reality?

In one particular experiment, Wiseman talks about two individuals, Brenda and Martin.

Martin considers himself lucky while Brenda considers her lot in life is destined to be adversely affected by misfortune. If it wasn't for bad luck, she wouldn't have any luck at all.

In the experiment, the two individuals are told to walk into a coffee shop to meet up with other people involved in the 'Luck' experiment.

What they don't know is the whole situation has been rigged.

On the doorstep of the shop is a crisp £20 note.

Inside the shop there are four tables and at one of the tables is sitting a successful businessman.

What do you think happens to Brenda as she walks into the shop?

Somehow, she manages to walk right over the £20 note and when inside the shop she keeps herself to herself and doesn't speak to anyone.

And Martin? Sure enough he glances down and true to form can't believe his good luck as he picks up the note. Once in the shop he makes the most of his good luck by striking up a conversation with the businessman and offers to buy him a coffee.

The same reality for the two people but very different results.

What the Thinker thinks the Prover proves!

Consider this for yourself.

Are you proud of your putting?

We have noticed over the years that there is more of an honour in being a good ball-striker than a good putter.

The 'he is a great ball-striker' story is delivered with a puffed-out chest and a sense of dramatic pride yet how often have we heard people say that such-and-such a player can't really hit it but get him on the greens and he is something of a 'blade merchant' – almost as if it is a lesser ability to be great on the greens.

People love to hear stories about legendary ball-strikers such as Ben Hogan and Mac O'Grady, then endlessly try to decipher their 'secrets' and become disciples of their methodologies.

Yet the same aura doesn't seem to be afforded to great putters such as Bobby Locke, Ben Crenshaw and Loren Roberts.

Could this theme have had an impact on certain players over the years?

For us, we need no convincing that some players will look back with a degree of regret on their career as a result of being less than they could have been on the greens – partly as a result of the story they bought into as to the ego-boosting value of ball-striking over the simple task of rolling the ball on the green.

What is your story? How have you constructed a narrative around what happens when you have a putter in your hand? How do you talk about your performance on the greens?

How do you talk about your putting with others – and perhaps more importantly with yourself?

What do you say to yourself when you putt well? Do you dismiss those days as flukes?

How do you explain the days when the ball just doesn't want to go in?

Consider how much the story you have carried around with you for so long might have held back your progress.

As a result of buying into this story, how have you held yourself back from what you could have achieved?

Do you want to keep with the same old story as you move forwards or could it perhaps be the time to take charge of a new script? Do you want to be the author of your own future story or do you want to keep following the same old script?

The great and extremely powerful concept around a story is that it can be changed.

The most important aspect to understand is unless you change your story – the narrative you continually tell yourself – then no matter how many times you change your putter or no matter how much work you do on your putting stroke, you will never see any lasting change. Stories are that powerful. They bind us to our own self-imposed reality.

Make sure you go to dinner with good putters.

You can begin to see exactly what Mr Penick was getting at.

Changing your story

From a practical perspective, it is very difficult to just decide to change your story one day. It is unlikely after a history of mistakes and misfortunes on the greens that you can suddenly tell yourself you are a great putter and believe it.

However, what you can do is first of all recognise the current story and make a commitment that you are going to begin a new more useful and empowering narrative.

There needs to be a bridge between the old story and the new version of yourself.

As a start point, you could begin to create a story that looked like this.

How about the story was that you had decided, from today, that you were going to learn how to be great on the greens? Is that possible? Could it be possible to learn how to be great on the greens? Now, just imagine if you embraced this concept and the Thinker and the Prover started to go to work.

You begin to tell yourself that you have started a journey of learning discovery and you are drawing a line under the past. From here on in, it is about learning to roll the ball into the hole on a regular basis. As the great author CS Lewis put it: "You can't go back and change the beginning but you can start where you are and change the ending."

So you begin to think this. You commit to it.

Now what is your Prover going to go in search of?

Exactly – evidence to support the idea you are learning to be great on the greens.

When you do a drill and you discover something useful, then this reinforces the new story. When you can sense a new way of being on the greens you reinforce the new story. The great benefit of this new 'learning' story is that it is not dependent instantly on an outcome you cannot control – like whether the ball drops into the cup. You can control your perception of learning.

If we try to believe a new story that we will hole everything then it only takes a bit of evidence to the contrary to kick you right back to the old story. Learning is different.

We can miss a bunch of putts but still have a great learning experience IF we are looking for that learning.

Seeing exactly how the hole size can be altered by having better pace control doesn't mean we have to hole them all but it is a great learning experience.

I can begin to notice learning.

As Dr Langer would say: "You become a mindful learner as opposed to mindlessly reacting in the same pre-programmed way."

Suddenly, instead of constantly looking to reinforce the story of how bad we are and only looking at the results, we can really start to notice the effect of a mind freed up from all of the technical nonsense. We can be open to sensing and feeling what happens within a good putt. We open the learning door and set the scene for performance to follow.

A helpful exercise: writing your story

Take some time out to do this, it is a VERY important exercise.

It has been proven to us many times the power of actually writing out the current story. When you see the way you currently construct your world down on paper it is then out of your head and you can really see it for what it is.

You then get to choose your story as opposed to just constantly playing out an automatic pre-programmed response. The Thinker and Prover can then go to work on a different script. Your script. Your own conscious choice as to the direction you wish to go. Write out your current story. Get yourself a notebook as this will be a very important aid to the progress you will make.

Details are the key. You want to have a very comprehensive view of the current limiting story. Write out:
• How you talk about your putting both to yourself and to others.
• How you view a putt when you walk onto the green
• How your view changes dependent on the length of the putt
• What kind of dialogue you have with yourself about a putt
• Whether it changes depending on whether you have a birdie putt or a par putt
• What feelings are attached to being on the putting surface
• How you react when you miss a putt
• How you react when you hole a putt
• How you talk about putting in general
• Whether you dismiss good putters or admire them?

Now write out your new story. Take yourself out into the future and describe how you will be different. How you will explain to yourself what happens on the greens in a way that allows you to learn to roll the ball towards the hole in the best way possible.

• How you are different with regards to your putting
• What you have done to make this happen
• How your conversation with yourself and others is different to how it used to be
• How it feels to be learning a new skill
• How you react when you hole a putt
• How you explain a missed putt to yourself
• How you explain a poor day on the greens to yourself
• What some of the things are that you will experience as you live out this new story
• How you look back on the way you used to be
• What the key differences are that you see, hear and feel
• How it feels to have changed such a limiting story

What you will have as you complete this exercise is a couple of very clear images for the brain to consider.

You see very clearly what will happen if you continue with the existing story. You see the consequences of continuing just as you are. You then create a compelling description of a totally different reality. You give yourself a blueprint of what to work towards.

When your brain has a clear idea of what not to do and has an even clearer road map of what to do, then you can create an incredible opportunity for lasting change and progress.

We are talking about putting here but just imagine how you could apply this principle in so many other areas of your life. You will be constructing stories that do not serve you well. You will be following a script in virtually all areas of your life as we act out life in a state of unconscious auto-pilot. You can keep the stories if you like or you can decide to change them. The choice is yours. You can choose to allow someone else to write it for you or you can choose to write your own story.

Key takeaways

1 A missed putt in and of itself means nothing beyond the meaning we personally attach to it.

2 Poor putters indulge in a 'pity party' of all the putts they have missed.
These stories become our reality. If we tell ourselves a story enough times we actually become the story.

3 Can you begin to see how your own narrative of your putting capability has such a long-term effect on your performance?

4 Consider how much the putting story you have carried around with you for so long might have held you back. Do you want to keep with the same old story or could it perhaps be the time to take charge of a new script?

5 You can keep the existing story or you can decide to change them. The choice is yours. You can choose to allow someone else to write it for you or you can choose to write your own story.

TRACKMAN AND PUTTING

FROM the very outset, we have maintained that putting is an art rather than a science. However, we are very aware that we need science to back up our concepts.

With that in mind, we enlisted the help of our good friends at TrackMan, internationally recognised as the industry leaders in club and ball data, whose orange radar devices are instantly recognisable the world over. We have worked very closely with TrackMan over the last few years and having spent some time with them at their HQ in Denmark, we knew that they would provide us and you, with some incredibly valuable insights.

As you will see, in this information, our colleagues at TrackMan reinforce that the single most important question to ask on the greens is "what does the ball need to do to go in the hole?"

TrackMan Performance Putting
With Trackman's Niklas Bergdahl

Let's face it, the only thing that really matters is what the ball is doing. It's as simple as that. Where the ball ends up is the result and where the performance is measured.

As an introductory comment, one of the under-appreciated pieces in the puzzle of making putts is the fact that the ball is rolling on the ground most of the time, making the surface a significant influencer on where the ball ends up.

On a more measurable level, the launch of the ball is what really dictates the outcome. The main influencers here are ball speed, launch direction, launch angle and launch spin.

In this regard, friction also has an impact, particularly when the ball is skidding.

In technical terms, skid happens when the ball's speed decelerates at a higher rate until the ground's friction makes the ball's rotation (peripheral speed) match the velocity of the ball. Once these two momentums are equal, the ball stops skidding and starts to roll. From then on, the putt becomes relatively predictable in terms of distance and break.

With this in mind, the player has a handful of parameters he can control or influence: The start line; the initial ball speed; and the distance to the ball's first touch of the ground.

Once the ball is on the ground, the physics of the surface takes over. Here, the player must try to understand how the rest of the putt will pan out, depending on the launch conditions the player "gave" the ball. The key here is to be capable of figuring out how direction and speed are affected during the skid phase, when the ball starts rolling, and at what speed.

Because of the higher deceleration during the skid phase, it is critical for the player to understand that initial ball speed is not the same for every putt, as it depends on distance and effective stimp or speed of the putting surface. It relies on the skid distance and the speed drop.

Without knowing these parameters for any given putt, the player cannot truly determine what pace is needed to achieve a given distance. Furthermore, the understanding of the initial speed behaviour will also affect the amount of break, and therefore also the line, which we will look into at a later point.

When it comes down to how players prepare for a given putt the process is very individual. However, there is basically only one fundamental question for the player to always answer: what does the ball need to do in order to end up in the hole, given that the hole is the ultimate target?

At TrackMan we've always started with focusing on tracking the outcome, which is the ball and the measured performance factor.

If you are forced to choose between looking at the ball or the club, the answer is always the ball. Isolating club delivery will never be sufficient to measure a player's ability to become a better putter. The reason behind this being the great influence the green surface has on the outcome. If all the greens were flat and had zero grain, had the same speed for all putts and the hole would capture the ball regardless of entry speed, then it would only come down to launch ball speed and direction. We know that's not the case, so why is such a great amount of putting practice focussing on basically only the face angle direction, impact location on the face and the speed of the club?

Another consequence of practising where isolated attention is on the club delivery in a controlled environment is that the player isn't trained to go through the correct pre-shot process and thus not capable of assessing the green's influence on the ball for any given putt before that putt is struck.

Once the putt has been struck, the player will be able to know how the ball will behave given the speed of this putt and, from there, any repeat of the same putt is simply practising the stroke mechanics.

If the player has been trained to acquire the necessary skill set to determine how the ball will behave for a given putt, only by assessing the distance of the putt and the speed, then that will be a key for making the best possible decision for the intended speed and intended starting direction.

It's probably human nature to question what you can control rather than where you have less control. That's most likely the reason you question or think about your stroke mechanics after the putt is executed. It can also be because this is the only thing you are focusing on in your practice. However, there are other factors that have higher importance on determining why the ball is ending up anywhere but in the hole.

First, if you truly don't know how the green will influence the direction and distance of the putt, you should never allow yourself to question your club delivery. Add uncertainty and lack of commitment and any proper technique will break down.

Most players don't understand that once the ball touches the ground on the first bounce at launch, they are in the hands of the green. The best players in the world are capable of starting the ball inside the hole repeatedly from 12 feet and together with their distance control – (based on ball speed consistency of 0.2 mph) – they should be capable of making 95 per cent at this distance. (Source Jon Karlsen 2010).

The reality on the PGA Tour is quite different as they make 96 per cent at three feet and 50 per cent at eight feet.

Why is that? Green-reading ability and situational tendencies, as well as green inconsistencies, are the most important ones. There is no question in our minds that there is potential to be unleashed here. This is essentially a combination of how players practice and the evaluation process for each and every putt they hit.

The correct way to look at a putt is to think about the end result, which comes down to how the ball should enter the hole. The ball's speed when it reaches the hole determines the effective size of the hole and therefore if it can enter it. The higher the speed of the ball, the more reduced the hole size will be. The main thing here is to determine the strategy of speed (and roll-out distance) should the ball not enter the hole with the correct direction.

TrackMan's performance parameter 'Break' is the amount of break (right or left) in relation to the launch direction. It's measured when ball speed is 0.7 m/s (1.68 mph). The reason for the break number to be measured at this particular speed is for players to use this number to understand where to start the ball.

Conventional thinking is to measure the break at the ball's resting position, but here the break number will be even bigger due to the increased break in the last part of the roll, where the ball should have entered the hole.

Back to the 0.7 m/s. This speed gives an effective hole size of 74 per cent and a potential roll-out of one foot at effective stimp of seven and at two feet at an effective stimp of 14. The key learning here is that ball speed at the hole is more important than the exact roll-out, as the latter is determined by the effective stimp of the green.

Now that we understand how the ball is supposed to enter the hole, we can discuss what initial ball speed is needed. There will be a window of initial ball speeds that will be possible in order to make the putt. This will create an imaginary cone of possible lines where the ball can roll to go into the hole.

The higher speed will have less break and could be referred to as the low side of the cone. The launch direction, in this case, will be closer to the hole compared to the lower ball speeds. This will, however, make the effective hole size smaller, plus leave a longer distance for the next putt, should it not go in. On the other hand, the lowest speed possible could be referred to the high side of the cone, and this will require a launch direction further away from the hole compared to the faster speeds.

This speed strategy will result in the largest effective hole size as the ball would reach the hole with as low speed as possible, making it more likely to drop into the hole, if it reaches the hole. Even though this speed could be argued as the ideal speed to just drop into the hole given the largest effective hole size, the ball is much more sensitive to green inconsistencies as it's reaching the hole, plus the fact the risk of leaving it short is higher.

Focusing on achieving entry speed of 0.7m/s has many benefits. In terms of distance control (consistency in achieving a certain a distance), even a putt that will be considered as launched with a lower speed can still reach the hole and with a lower speed this can also achieve a larger effective hole size, presuming the direction matches the speed.

Furthermore, this strategy could also be seen as less aggressive and the distance of the next putt, in the likelihood that the ball doesn't go in, should not be as long.

Ultimately, it all comes down to the fact that there are combinations of launch directions and speeds that can make the ball go into the hole. Even with unintentional error in direction and speed, the ball can still go in the hole using a different line than was originally decided upon.

One of the things that is always tough to communicate is to stop focussing on whether the putt was made or not.

As mentioned earlier, the correct coordination between speed and direction can still make the putt go in the hole, even if it wasn't executed according to the player's intention. This doesn't mean that putting practice shouldn't include a hole. The point is that you need accurate feedback on direction, speed, skid, roll and break before you can truly assess if the putt was executed according to the intention.

A crucial part of putting performance comes down to the player's ability to predict:

The effective stimp

The speed needed to reach the hole with desired entry speed

The amount of break this speed will lead to, thus giving the launch direction for the putt.

In reality, this needs to be broken down into segments that the player can practise in order to become consistent in club delivery and skilful in understanding how to predict effectively the ball's interaction with the ground.

This will lead to predictability for any given putt and ultimately equipping the player with the ability to become adaptable to situations. The skill of adaptability is fundamental to putting performance, as golf is played with a big factor of randomness.

The player needs to practise the ability to start the ball on line, which is launch direction zero, relative to the intended start line at different distances and in different slope conditions. This will make the situational tendencies transparent.

Using this type of practice, the player will soon learn to start the ball on the line regardless of distance and slope.

Over and above that, achieving a desired ball and roll speed on different distances and surface conditions is essential. Ball speed is determined by the club speed, the impact location and club head weight plus COR. Club speed is primarily determined by the forward swing time and the stroke length.

Roll speed is a consequence of the ball speed and the skid distance. The skid distance is determined by the ball speed, the launch angle of the ball and the launch spin as well as the green conditions and effective stimp. This is determined by club speed, dynamic loft and impact location.

Another important factor is the role and understanding of the surface you are putting on. Going from indoor or to outdoor has a big impact on putts, as real greens are very different from artificial grass.

The majority of the artificial greens on the market are not 'simulating' real green grass, and the ball will therefore not behave the same way.

Further, even on real grass, the conditions may vary quite a bit, and the player and coach must possess a good knowledge of how certain green conditions will affect the outcome. Having a system that is capable of mapping the green conditions is therefore crucial.

Lastly, a great example of how to understand the surface's influence on the ball is to take a very consistent player and compare the speed, skid, roll, break and distance outdoors versus indoors.

This will help to 'translate' the numbers and will give a good indication of what are considered 'good numbers'. Especially as the skid distance will vary according to surface conditions. This will help you practise in different conditions and still understand the player's true performance.

Niklas Bergdahl

How TrackMan has changed the way golf is viewed, coached and played

TrackMan technology and intuitive software is a significant milestone in the evolution of golf instruction, coaching, fitting, and entertainment. Conclusive data is delivered in an easy-to-understand format, empowering professionals to excel in their training routines. The end product is a suite of extremely tailored programs that fit any player at any level.

Since the start, the TrackMan product and name has become the gold standard for club delivery and ball flight measurements and has been used on the PGA Tour since 2006. The TrackMan product has evolved from a R&D tool to a club fitting tool and now the most coveted teaching tool in golf. The website **mytrackman.com** allows the golfer to take advantage of the data and information collected.

Recently, TrackMan has launched major updates to the portfolio through TrackMan Performance Studio 6.0, where new possibilities arise in a merged world of practice, entertainment, and virtual golf in a world of hyper-realistic golf courses that lets you play or practice real golf with real distances. True to our philosophy of being non-intrusive and out of sight when a ball is struck, no markers or external aids are needed to capture this critical information.

The TrackMan numbers are the brains behind it all. All major stakeholders of the game, without exception, use and trust our numbers for two main reasons: precision and reliability.

With TrackMan, you will quickly understand why and how they use our data in their daily work. With us, you'll quickly become an insider of the most revolutionary training tool in the industry.

TrackMan tracks the full trajectory of any shot, from 10-feet putts to six-foot chips to 400-yard drives, pin-pointing the landing position with an accuracy of less than one foot at 100 yards.

We also display the shot's 3D trajectory together with 30 impact and ball flight parameters in real time (data is delivered within one second). Add to that, the capability of measuring the only technology to track the full ball roll in putting, together with club data as well as synchronised high-speed video.

Today, 84 of the top 100 PGA Tour players have purchased their own TrackMan. A total of more than 700 of the players on the top tours globally are TrackMan owners, with a constant growth.

Top coaches, national teams, top amateurs, universities and serious golfers around the world are all trusting TrackMan.

If you go to a PGA or European Tour event, the driving range is crowded with TrackMan units giving precise feedback to the majority of the players, every single week, year after year.

Today, TrackMan is considered to be the world leader in sports ball measurement, and the company has become the industry standard for accuracy in both golf and baseball. TrackMan A/S is a privately held Danish company, established in 2003.

To discover how TrackMan can help accelerate your learning process and make practice more fun, visit **trackman.com**

Chapter 2
ATTENTION

WHAT are you doing right now? Yes, you! Are you really here with us?

Or are you just glancing at this book and scanning the information waiting to see if you find something that will instantly fix all of your putting issues?

How quickly could you be distracted and taken away from us?

What if your phone beeps with another one of those oh-so-important alerts?

Would you be able to stay here with us or would we lose you to another video of a cat playing with a ball of string?

Unfortunately, most of us are in a constant state of low-level distraction. Our attention is literally hopping from one thing to another all through the day.

Then we attempt to play a game like golf which absolutely demands our attention to be here and now on the task at hand.

What is it we find so engaging about things that don't really engage us? Why do we treat this wonderful piece of machinery we have between our ears with such little respect and, more importantly, are we any happier for it?

What has gone so wrong with the simple ability just to be present in something for a period of time?

In his wonderful book, The Hijacking of the American Mind, Robert Lustig explains how we can gain a rush of the neurotransmitter dopamine to the brain when we go on Facebook and get a like.

The problem being, dopamine can become addictive. We crave the high it gives us and, like all addictions, we need more and more to fuel the sense of need.

It is as if our brain begins to crave these short-term hits and fixes of instant social media gratification. The more we get the more we want. But what price are we paying for this?

This craving for attention from others and the distraction this causes actually plays havoc with the attention that really matters – your own attention to what is truly important to you.

Lustig talks about the difference between dopamine and serotonin. Dopamine is the pleasure driver and the more we get the more we want. Serotonin, however, is more of a driver of happiness and contentment. Serotonin, paradoxically, isn't an instant hit but tends to create a sense of satisfaction because you have been absorbed in a challenging activity like a gym session, solving a complex problem or being fully engaged in a practice session.

The reason we mention this is we firmly believe great putting, and indeed great golf, comes from your ability to pay attention.

Becoming aware of where your attention is

In Karl's previous book, Attention – The Secret to You Playing Great Golf, he explains that your attention is always in one of two places for the task or goal at hand.

You will either have your attention on something useful to you, or you will allow your attention to drift off in the direction of something that is useless. So simple yet so important.

Attention on something useful to the task you want to perform or useless to that task.

For many golfers, unfortunately, most of the time our precious attention has been drawn into the useless box.

We spend so many hours attempting to train our body to make a 'correct' stroke yet how much time do we ever spend aiming to train our attention?

Yet we can promise you that if you are not holing the putts you wish to then this issue will have, to a large degree, attention right at the heart of the problem.

To even begin to make progress with this, there is a key question you can begin ask yourself: What is my attention on?

To simply ask the question allows us to enjoy a uniquely human skill which is to be able to go 'meta', or above, our thinking. We can become aware of the content of our thoughts.

We can watch or observe our thinking.

The problem for most of us is that our habitual thinking is just that – habitual. We constantly engage endless loops of largely useless thoughts. It has been stated that we have anywhere up to 80,000 thoughts per day and it would be fair to say most of those thoughts you will be having today are just a recycled version of the thoughts you had yesterday.

Most of those thoughts will revolve around a fairly simple axis. You will be concerned about things you have not done, things you should have done or things you regret doing.

Or you will be looking in the house of the close-thought relation of what do I need to do, what should I be doing, what am I not doing, I wonder if it will all turn out ok for me. I am sure you get the picture.

So much thinking which actually prevents an awful lot of doing. We have this time machine in our head constantly playing tricks on us. By default, some people are more mired in the past while others are constantly worried about the future. This time machine has a useful purpose if we take a little bit more ownership of it.

The past does have a purpose and a use for us; the future is there to be embraced and to a degree planned for.

But for the most part this endless time travelling is doing nothing other than robbing us of the only time we have any kind of control over: the present moment.

What you have right here and now is really all there is. In actual reality the past doesn't exist, it is just a conversation you are having with yourself in this moment about a past event and by the same measure nor does the future. It is just a conversation you are having with yourself in the moment about a potential experience that hasn't happened yet.

It is crazy but so many of us are literally walking around inside of our head all day long. We are not experiencing the world through our senses and yet when we come to try to hole a putt one thing is for sure: we need to be VERY tuned in to our senses. It could be argued that we have become mindless instead of mindful.

To quote the therapist Fritz Perls: "We need to stop thinking and come to our senses."

There is a captivating video on YouTube of a player we have worked with in the past, the former Ryder Cup captain Paul McGinley, talking about the putt he holed to win the Ryder Cup at The Belfry in 2002.

Watch the piece again as it is a summary lesson in the power of having your attention in a useful place.

McGinley could have walked onto that green with the gravity of the situation weighing him down. He knew his match was crucial in a tight contest. He could have considered it was he who may have a putt to win the Ryder Cup. He could have considered just how many people would be watching the action live, all around the world. He could have put his attention on the possibility of the shame of 'losing' the Ryder Cup. However, he didn't.

In the video, McGinley talks about how he became absorbed in the putt itself. He talks about feeling the pace of the putt. He dismisses his caddie away as he knows what he has got to do with this particular task of rolling a ball some 10 feet towards the hole. He even describes how the slope became so apparent he felt like he hooked the putt into the slope.

The feeling with his hands is so acute, so clear. All of his language describing this putt is sensory-based. He is tuned into his senses. The senses are based here and now in this moment and not mired in some far-flung pretend place we call the past or the future.

It is a masterclass in attention and the near-miraculous events that can materialise when we put our attention in a place useful to us.

As a contrast, look at perhaps the most famous missed putt of all time. The more you watch it, the more uncomfortable the viewing is.

The scene takes us back to the final green at St Andrews in 1970. Doug Sanders is crouched over a putt to change his life.

Clad in matching purple sweater, slacks and shoes, he is faced with a putt of less than three feet. He sets up to putt and then something catches his eye on his line. Without resetting and going back through his process he sets up again.

As the ensuing putt drifts agonisingly past the hole, the late Henry Longhurst utters the immortal words: "And there but for the grace of God." If you watch the video, and we recommend you do, but only once, you will see Sanders' stroke. Everything seems to be moving as he looks like he is trying to pick the ball out of the hole before he has even hit the putt. We often ask people up and down the country in the putting seminars we do, given this putt was to win the Open: "Could Doug Sanders' putting stroke been as bad as this for the previous 71 holes?" Everyone answers – of course not. So in that white-heat moment did Sanders have a putting issue or an attention issue?

It is easy for us to say but it would seem that, unlike McGinley, who was totally absorbed in the putt itself, Sanders was very much focused on what the putt was for as opposed to the task of rolling the ball along a certain line at a certain pace.

It is a tragic scene and too many people only remember Sanders for this snapshot of what was a great career. He is one of a select group of players who has won 20 events or more on the PGA Tour. He also made a great up and down from the Road Hole bunker on the 17th to get into this position. Yet the only thing most people tend to remember is that missed putt.

Apparently, Doug Sanders was asked a few years ago if the putt still bothered him. No, he said, nowhere near as much as it used to do. He can go at least an hour these days without thinking about it!

We firmly believe many putts are missed well before we get anywhere near our ball as a result of the maelstrom of thinking going on in our heads. Anxious thoughts create anxious responses. Just by the way we think, we can activate our sympathetic nervous system. The ancient hard- wired response we have to danger or perceived threat. The response that says either fight this thing or run away. If it occurs to us that this putt is the golf equivalent of life or death then our bodies will respond to that perceived threat.

As part of a sympathetic nervous system response our pupils will dilate, our heart rate increases and we sweat more. None of these responses are useful for putting.

If it occurs to us that this putt is why we are here, this is our house, this is our home and we really want to be here, then the body's response and the ability to carry out that task will be hugely improved.

How Breathing Can Help Your Attention

Patrick McKeown is the author of a wonderful book called The Oxygen Advantage. He talked about the profound benefits of simply bringing your attention to your breath throughout the day.

Just by simply bringing your attention to your breath you quieten the mind. You activate the parasympathetic nervous system, your relaxation response. You put your mind and body in a state to receive information that the green and the putt will be giving you.

When the sympathetic system is on full tilt, your ability to read line and feel pace will be dramatically reduced.

How many people have said 'I just couldn't read the putt' yet how many would ever consider that the walk up to the green and the accompanying thoughts actually were a direct contribution as to why they struggled to read the putt?

This is not new. These ideas have been around for thousands of years and are central to most of the martial arts and disciplines such as yoga. Could it be that the walk from your approach to the green is an opportunity?

It is an opportunity to get lost in thought – past or future – what may or may not be. Or it could be the opportunity to create the mental conditions to allow yourself to hole a putt. To receive the information the green is trying to give you.

The walk on to the green can either set you up to feel anxiety and dread or it could be an opportunity to place your attention in a place you personally find to be really useful. Time and time again with players who think their stroke is at fault, we have had real and lasting success by simply getting them to work on their 'walk' up to the green.

Just imagine now if you made a commitment as you walk up to the green you simply place your attention on your breath.

Most importantly, you breathe in and out through the nose.

You do not attempt to take a deep breath in through the mouth heaving your shoulders up at the same time, as this will only serve to increase any tension levels.

You are aiming to slow down the breath gently as you inhale and exhale through the nose. You may notice your mind wandering to what the putt may be for or you drift back to the putts you have just missed but you notice this and gently just allow your focus of attention to your nose breathing.

At the very least this is a wonderful exercise to train your attention. You are in effect meditating while you are walking.

You are deciding to put your attention in a place you deem to be useful. You are quietening the mind while at the same time grounding yourself in the present moment.

Many players report back that this is a deeply satisfying exercise. It actually feels good to be present.

The walk itself becomes a pleasure for its own sake.

You may not find the time to formally meditate but you get exactly the same benefit by doing this exercise. The science on meditation is very strong – it has been proven to be good for you.

As a very pleasant side effect to all of that healthy benefit, we believe you will be pleasantly surprised at the effect on your putting. You may begin to notice when you do this that as you walk onto the green you start to get a sharper, in-focus look and feel of the slopes and undulations of the greens. Your ability to visualise the line and pace of the putt improves. All of this is because with 'the walk' you are so much more in tune with your body as opposed to being lost in your head.

As you are more tuned in to your body you are synchronising your system to take in the relevant information to which you need to hole the putt. You can even extend and practise this idea in your general life.

When you are in the car on a long journey instead of listening to more nonsense on the radio just keep your eyes on the road but allow your mind to focus on the rise and fall of your breath as you breathe quietly through your nose.

As you are walking down the street, instead of being 'lost in thought' just simply be aware of the rise and fall of your breath; or you could notice the feeling of your feet as they hit the ground, the rise and fall of the foot.

Far from this being just idle daydreaming you are actually training your mind to potentially hole more putts. It may seem crazy but the science on the benefits of this is sound.

The ability to quieten the mental chatter and just be present to something physical that is happening right here and now. Most people who do this report back that far from being a waste of time it is actually an inherently pleasurable experience.

They experience a mental de-clutter which leads to fantastic clarity by taking time out from the constant distraction of their devices and all of the 'shoulds' and 'musts' the mind throws up.

Five exercises

Exercise 1: Attention on the breath

Give yourself the task for the next 21 days that you are going to spend some part of each day just simply being with and noticing your breath.

Put a note somewhere you can see first thing in the morning that simply says 'Check in with the breath!'

You could be in the car, taking a walk or being in a queue at the supermarket. The great thing is you can practise this anywhere.

Simply bring your attention to the rise and fall of your breath. Make sure you are breathing in and out through your nose. But just simply be with the breath without trying to change anything. It is the observing that is the key. You may notice or you will notice that your attention drifts to other things. That is fine, that is what the mind does. But just notice and gently bring your attention back to the rise and fall of your breath. Don't fall into the trap of thinking it is all about keeping your attention on the breath and anything else is failure.

The great learning from this is to notice the mind wandering and then having the ability to bring it back: notice, bring back, notice, bring back.

You may find this exercise a real challenge at first or you may instantly feel a sense of profound calm or peace spreading over you as your mind settles instead of jumping from one attention post to another.

It may seem the strangest thing that you can actually improve your putting standing in a line in a shop but you can.

You are doing what so very few people do, you are training your attention, you are noticing your attention, you are becoming aware of what your mind habitually engages in as it spends the day jumping around in a state of constant low level distraction.

Create a spreadsheet or make a note in your diary. If you do this on any given day even for a few moments, you simply give yourself a tick. Job done for the day.

Exercise 2: The Walk

Make a commitment for the next 10 rounds you play.

Every time you hit a green, as you approach the putting surface simply come back to your breathing.

Obviously, if you have hit a 3-iron in then the walk will be a little longer than if you have just pitched on from 50 yards but the principle remains the same. The key time to engage is from 10 yards off the putting surface. The time when you would perhaps normally immerse yourself in all of the stories about the putt you have facing you.

Instead of engaging in those stories, have the discipline just to be with the breath for the short walk and as you first step onto the green.

As before, your mind will wander to what this means and how much you need to hole the putt but just let the stories be and gently bring your attention back to the breath.

For many players who do this they find it very calming and it creates a great 'state' to receive the information the green is providing them.

The green gives you all you need to know, you just have to be ready to receive it.

Mark this on your scorecard. Give yourself a tick after every hole you do it. Eighteen ticks is a perfect mental game score. Eighteen ticks tells you that you have done all you can to hole the putt REGARDLESS of the outcome.

Exercise 3: The after-image

Here is a question we always ask our students during our putting schools: When was the last time you saw something for the first time that has always been there?

If, like the majority of our students, you now have a puzzled look on your face as you try to make sense of this strange enquiry then bear with us. Many things we see throughout our day are just filtered through the lens of 'I have seen that before' so we go on auto-pilot and we notice very little of what is actually there.

As Dr Ellen Langer says: "We are just not there." We are often mindless as opposed to being mindful.

Putting is no exception and the exercise we are about to share with you that we learned from Fred Shoemaker will really highlight this as well as provide you with an experience that can really make you a better and more successful putter.

So here goes. Take a single golf ball. Go out on to a green and kneel down.

Put the ball on to the putting surface and focus on the ball. Really look at the ball.

What do you see?

You will obviously see 'Titleist' or 'Callaway' or whatever but as you look at the ball notice that some of it will be brighter than other parts.

Some parts of the ball will be in shade. Some will highlight the natural light. Focus intently on one dimple and imagine you are looking right through the ball.

Now take the ball between your thumb and first finger. Quickly snatch the ball away and keep looking where the ball used to be on the green. What do you see?

If you focus, you will see a round blur, a fuzzy impression of where the ball once was, a dark circle. This is what is known as a retinal after-image.

It is not unlike when you look at a lightbulb, close your eyes and you can still see the image of the light. Have you ever seen this image before?

For most people it is a total surprise to see this image. Especially when we tell them that image has been there on every single putt they have ever hit in their life before and they have never seen it! Now, if you have never seen it before what does it say about the location of your attention?

How quickly does your attention jump to the outcome? Did it go in? Did I make it or miss it? Was my putting stroke ok?

Would there have been any possible chance that Doug Sanders would have seen the after-image on that fateful putt on the 18th at

St Andrews? Highly unlikely.

Now, what we want you to do is simply take your golf ball and putt.

Not to a target. Just send the ball out there. Your only goal is to see the after-image. Many golfers when they try this for the first time report back on how calm they feel.

They talk about how their stroke feels smooth and how pure the strike was. Yet we have done nothing to work on their technique. We have simply changed their attention from something 'useless' to 'useful'.

Exercise 4: Playing with the after-image

Now to extend this a little further. Keep aiming to 'see' the after-image but now we want you to introduce the hole into the equation.

Same goal though – all we want you to do is to see the after-image. Notice if the quality of the image remains the same when you introduce the hole.

Does it stay the same or does the introduction of the hole weaken your intention to keep your attention on the after-image?

Now, on short putts in particular, after you have set up and you have one of those putts that in the past would have caused you an issue in your previous story, we are giving you a new goal.

Your goal is to simply see the after-image.

If the ball goes in, it goes in. If it misses, it misses.

As long as you have seen the after-image you have done your bit. You have chosen to put your attention in a certain place and you have kept it there for the duration of the putt.

Suddenly the goal changes from an outcome you cannot control, holing the putt, to a process you have control over. The by-product we see time and time again in our schools is that when you focus on observing the after-image an awful lot of very pleasant technical side effects show up.

You stay down on the putt; the strike is pure and centred; your stroke is smooth – it is natural and flowing because you are not trying to control it. As your attention is focused on the after-image your mind goes quiet and allows your body to take over and do what it is trained to do.

When doing this exercise, give yourself marks out of 10 for how clear the after-image is, ten being very vivid.

You may or not be surprised to discover there is a direct correlation between how good your attention is and how many putts you hole.

"In 2003 I was putting poorly mainly because I had a habit of following the putter head in the backswing which lead to all sorts of issues. I improved this by focussing my attention on the front middle of the ball, then my intention was to hit through this point. It freed up my mind and my stroke and kept my eyes and attention on the ball and not the putter. The following eight seasons, I was in the top 10 in both putts per rounds and putts per green in regulation on the European Tour.

"I'm not blessed with a consistent swing like Bernhard Langer, but when it's on it's on, it works. If I'm putting well then anything can happen."

– Paul Broadhurst, Ryder Cup player, winner of six European Tour events and several Senior/Champions Tour events including the 2016 Senior Open Championship at Carnoustie and the 2018 Senior PGA Championship at Harbor Shores.

Exercise 5: Using the after-image before you play.

It is all well and good to talk about your attention being in a useful place when life itself is doing everything it possibly can to distract us.

How often do we attempt to play golf with so much 'noise' in our heads? We rush from work or home with so much going on.

Our mobile phone is constantly chirping and wanting to grab our attention on the next piece of social media trivia.

It can often seem like we are halfway through a round before we do finally tune into the game itself and the surroundings we are in.

From a score perspective this can often be far too late and the chance of a decent round is lost.

Many players try to do some stretching exercise before they play, some will even go and hit some balls on the range but how many actually ever think about tuning in and settling their attention on this moment?

To be able to still the mind and be mentally ready for golf is a tremendous advantage.

We have found the after-image is wonderful for this.

If you do nothing else to get your mind ready for golf then promise us that you will go to the putting green before your play and simply roll a few balls out onto the green and just simply observe the image.

No other goal.

Just let the putter flow back and through and see the image.

It is like a five-minute mental decompression before you play.

You are choosing to let the world be what it will be while you hold your attention on something that is here and now. Not in a past that you can't do anything about or a future that hasn't happened yet but just simply on the here and now.

Key takeaways

1 We spend so many hours attempting to train our body to make a 'correct' stroke yet how much time do we ever spend aiming to train our attention?

2 Many putts are missed well before we get anywhere near our ball as a result of the maelstrom of thinking going on in our heads.

3 The walk on to the green can either set you up to feel anxiety and dread or it could be an opportunity to place your attention in a place you personally find to be really useful.

4 By breathing in and out through the nose you are in effect meditating while you are walking. You are deciding to put your attention in a place you deem to be useful. You are quietening the mind while at the same time grounding yourself in the present moment.

5 Practise using the retinal after-image to feel calm on the greens. It will make your stroke feel smooth and your striking pure. It will move your attention from something useless to something useful.

GOLF'S DEADLIEST DISEASE: THE YIPS

THERE can be few sporting afflictions as deadly and debilitating as the yips.

We have seen many players driven to the point of despair when their mind and body seem to be completely at odds with each other faced with a simple task of rolling a ball towards a hole.

Careers have been either cut short or ruined by this seemingly strange phenomenon.

If you have never been afflicted then some of the descriptions of the yips can seem very odd.

We have worked with many players over the years who suffer with the problem. At its worst, it can look as though someone has just been prodded with an electrical charge as they try to move the putter through the ball.

It is not a pleasant sight but much of the issue is compounded by myth and downright bad information.

The old adage used to be that 'if you've had 'em you've got 'em!' – meaning that once you had suffered the wrath of the golfing gods and got the yips there was nothing you could do about it.

We believe this is fundamentally wrong and that you can and will recover if you have been suffering from this problem on the greens.

We can say with some pride that some of our most satisfying coaching moments have been with players who have staged a full yip recovery and get back to enjoying the game in the way they deserve.

Much research has been done on the yips.

Brain imaging, laboratory testing, you name it – it has been done over the past 20 years. The research does shed some light on the origination of the problem but perhaps far more importantly on what some of the solutions may actually be.

Here are some notes from our colleague and friend Debbie Crews who has done as much research as anyone surrounding the yips.

• Yips in putting increases 18-hole scores by an average of 4.5 strokes per round (The Yips, Smith et al, 2000).
• Yips can be divided into a minimum of two categories: neurological and psychological. A third category can be added when considering all the golfers in the grey area in between the two categories (Smith, et al., 2003).
• Neurological yips are more commonly known as: focal dystonia. This group is likely to account for 30 per cent or less of all yips golfers since this is similar to the prevalence of focal dystonia in the normal population.
• Psychologically induced yips tend to be conditional (only in certain situations), intermittent (off and on over time), or both. Anxiety is not correlated with performance among yips-affected golfers (Adler, Crews, Hentz, Smith, & Caviness, 2005). Anxiety exacerbates the condition but it is not the cause.

It is so very interesting to hear that a relatively small amount of golfers have a neurological basis to their yips; and that anxiety can make the condition worse but is not the cause of the yips.

So above anything else the message is that there is more than enough hope that you can work with this issue and get back to enjoying your game again.

The yips is a cause close to our hearts because we firmly believe that golf can literally keep a person alive in their later years.

For someone who has perhaps suffered a bereavement or is lonely, golf can and does provide a social lifeline and a purpose.

The physical, mental and emotional challenges golf provides are good for us – not to mention the benefits of social interaction and connection with nature.

The yips can stop many players playing this wonderful game but, as you will read here, this definitely does not have to be the case.
– Dr Debbie Crews. Learn more at **myoptibrain.com**

Seven fixes for the yips

1) Change the action

It is no coincidence that many players, such as Bernhard Langer, have been able to overcome the yips with a radical change in the way that they hold the club.

Grips such as the 'claw', 'cack handed' and the 'broomhandle' make sense because you are basically recruiting a new set of neurons to perform the task. You are developing in effect a new motion requiring the brain to learn a new skill as opposed to continuing trying to operate a faulty programme with your old grip.

This should be the first port of call in your quest to fix the yips. Change your grip – and the more dramatically you change it the better.

It is important to then see the new grip as the start of a new 'story'. Remember the concept of thinker and prover? See this as the start of learning a new skill as opposed to just 'fixing' the yips. If you see it as a skill you are learning then you will be able to deal with the inevitable setbacks along the way.

If you see it as a 'fix' for the yips then you will be only one bad feeling on one single putt away from thinking that this new action doesn't work. You are learning not fixing.

2) Separate the hands

Physically separating the hands on the club changes the putting stroke from what is known as a unimanual activity to a bimanual task which is processed differently in the brain. This technique can also be beneficial for chipping and even the full swing.

This method can be seen by the brain as a completely different way to start a project, allowing for new patterns to form. It is as though you are learning a new skill as opposed to repairing something perceived to be broken.

3) Don't look at the ball

This may seem counter-intuitive but it would seem that an over-emphasis on looking at the ball can actually exaggerate the instance of yipping.

When we stare intently at something it can cause a huge increase in muscle tightness almost as if the system senses a danger activating the 'fight or flight' response, neither of which is particularly useful on a putting green.

By shifting our attention from the ball or the stroke itself, this can allow the brain and body to work more instinctively.

We have seen real progress with some yippers simply by getting them to look up and focus on a point beyond the ball.

It may feel strange at first but time and time again we see the stroke immediately becoming smooth again as there is no sense of an impending impact and the corresponding twitch.

Also, following Jordan Spieth's lead and actually looking at the hole instead of the ball can allow the stroke to release. Again, there is no impact anticipation.

4) Focus on the completion of the motion

Padraig Harrington once said, with a certainty only he can muster, that of all the swing thoughts or cues, the single most effective one he had encountered was to focus on a smooth, balanced finish.

It would seem that if we have the intention to finish in balance then the brain body system will organise the movement around that intent.

All the motion through impact will fall into place in the right sequence if we aim to finish correctly. And so it seems with the yips. We have worked with a number of players who made great progress by first of all pre programming where a good putting stroke would finish.

How it would look and feel and then to go ahead and actually make the stroke.

Again, this takes away the focus and anticipation of impact and allows the stroke to pass through the ball rather than at the ball. Take your practice stroke and really feel your finish position and then simply step into the ball and aim to repeat the motion.

5) Focus on the breath

Often the yips can be caused by the system 'jamming' – a result of too much technical input. Over the years we have seen too many careers ruined as a result of getting so involved in the development of a 'sound stroke'.

We focus our precious attention on rocking the shoulders, keeping the wrists firm, smooth acceleration, changing the path to a slight arc, making sure the blade is approaching the ball with an upward motion…

The list goes on and on. A very simple action of moving an implement in your hands backwards and forwards is blighted by the interference of the conscious mind in the desire to look good by some technical definition. When we get so technically involved with how to move the putter not only do we get totally detached from the process of holing putts but the yips can often lurk in the background as we drown in technical overload.

This technical overload can then often be compounded by a huge increase in tension levels.

One effective method to overcome this if the scenario is familiar to you is to focus your attention (yes, that word attention again) on your breath. Focus on making a smooth breathing rhythm through your nose.

Play around with it, but what seems to work really well is to get set behind the ball and then slowly and gently release your breath through the nose and at the point of full release just let the putter swing back and through.

As your conscious mind becomes super-occupied with the releasing of the breath, the unconscious motor programme is left alone to operate the putter back and through. The nice by-product of this is that as you focus on the breath you also tend to allow your tension levels to settle down to a point where you are much better able to function.

6) Thought suppression

Counting backwards, for example, will keep the frontal cortex busy and perhaps allow a better motion to occur.

Set yourself the task of starting at a certain number such as five and focus your conscious attention on simply counting down to one.

As you are absorbed in this task, then the motor programme is free to swing the putter.

Distraction – thinking of something other than our problem – can allow us to find a solution as it now has a chance to emerge or appear to us rather than taking hours of rumination trying to figure it out.

7) Change your Intention

If your intention of trying to make a silky-smooth stroke isn't working for you, it makes no sense to continue with that particular concept or intention.

As we have mentioned elsewhere, if trying to create a technically perfect stroke rarely provides the results you are looking for, go to work on creating putts rather than strokes.

Think about what the ball needs to do rather than what you and your putter need to do – it is a pretty radical departure from your norm.

This change of concept and intention once more allows you to start a new process of learning, therefore enabling you to leave the past behind and embark on a new and exciting adventure.

As Debbie Crews has pointed out, it is very important to have more than one tool in your yips bag. You can begin to work with the suggestions we have made but for us, the single most important aspect is the attitude that you bring to the changes.

If you think that you can try one of the techniques mentioned and the yips will just disappear then you will be one shot and one bad feeling away from square one. Do not view this as a zero-sum game.

Remember the thinker and the prover.

If you are looking for a 'cure' that will take all of the nasty feelings away then you will be disappointed. However, if you view this as learning a new skill and you are exploring some options then you will keep up with the learning process.

On a scale of 1 to 10, with 1 being no yip feeling at all and 10 being the full hit, as you develop these options you will find yourself being able to head towards one but a sudden bad feeling and a 10 doesn't mean you stop learning.

Be interested in where you sit on the 1-to-10 scale as you explore various options.

Note your progression and realise that, no matter what, you will still get some putts that do feel very uncomfortable. This is part of the process of recovery. The key is to stay with the process, reinforce your successes and let the poor putts reside where they belong – in the past.

A short story

"I first visited Gary and Karl because I had real issues with my putting. I had developed a tremor in my right hand standing over my putts. I had become obsessed with making a textbook-perfect putting stroke and was terrified of getting it wrong.

"They suggested I focus on what the ball needed to do rather than what I needed to do. Almost immediately, I started holing putts and the tremor in my right hand disappeared.

"So much so, I forgot I ever had one! I won trophies in the next two competitions I played in thanks to my putting and now consider myself to be a good putter. And that's something I never thought I would say."
Colin Ramsay

Chapter 3
TWO QUESTIONS

CAN you hear that noise in the background? I am sure you can now! Sorry about that, but we have both just experienced one of the absolute fundamentals of this book.

To quote the great motivational speaker Tony Robbins: "The quality of your life will be determined by the quality of your questions."

Or in our case: "The quality of your putting will be determined by the quality of your questions."

When we first heard that phrase many years ago at a Robbins seminar we didn't understand the gravity and importance of the statement – but we do now.

We have discussed how attention is vital to becoming the best on the greens you can be. One of the royal roads to better attention is to understand the value of questions. Questions focus your attention.

We make no apologies for the fact we have mentioned this before and will mention it again.

The reason is simple, to reinforce the importance of this statement: Questions focus our attention.

So, if questions focus our attention and we aim to control our attention to useful places then surely it becomes of vital importance when we are on the greens that we make sure to ask a couple of quality questions.

The ability to ask better questions can have a such a dramatic effect on the way we putt, not to mention the way we move through life in general. A good question is like a magnet for our attention. We are question answering machines. We cannot stop ourselves from answering questions. What does your best friend look like?

There, we are sure we have got you again!

You will have left this book for a moment and now you are thinking about your best friend. Nice, but perhaps not altogether useful at this very moment.

If we were about to sit down in one of the best restaurants in London or New York and we looked at you with a quizzical expression and said "there is something strange here, what do you think is wrong with this place?" your brain, left unchecked, would go in search of the answer and would more than likely come up with a perfectly plausible answer.

We seek to answer questions. Questions hold our attention, they direct our thinking. You can either utilise this wonderful phenomenon or you can just simply let it run you.

In the main, golfers ask dreadful questions: Why are these greens so slow? Why are they so bumpy? Why is play so slow? Will I ever hole another putt? Why is my putting so poor today?

The poor quality of our questions means by default our attention tends to be directed to useless places.

We ask poor questions as a matter of habit.

Poor questions assist poor attention and poor attention will help you to miss a whole bunch of putts.

One of the key things to understand is there is a big difference between asking positive questions and 'trying' to think positive.

Thinking positive often involves a statement about a future event that we make a prediction about.

'I am going to hole this putt' is a very positive statement.

'I am really going to hole it!'

'I am sure I am going to hole it.'

We can make this statement over and over in our mind to try to convince ourselves of something we probably don't really believe.

This tends to create a very busy mind as the past raises its ugly head and after telling ourselves we are going to hole the putt another voice chimes in to remind you of all the putts you have already missed today.

You can end up with a kind of internal war: telling yourself you can while simultaneously doubting yourself.

Often a golfer will start out a round making a lot of positive statements: It will be my day today, I am going to play great, I think I will hole everything.

For some, this strategy may work. However, in our experience a lot of players make those positive statements with the best of intentions but then reality takes over. The game kicks us in the teeth, we miss a bunch of putts and then many players will flip completely to the other side and just cave in to the negative and it becomes 'I can't hole anything'. Resignation often sets in and another day of opportunity on the golf course is lost forever.

It is this constant mental tennis match back and forth from positive to negative that is so very draining as the mind is lost in its own maelstrom of thinking.

Surely there has to be a better way. What about a way of being that you can stick with? A way of being that begins on the 1st green and only runs out when you either decide to let it run out or you hole your last putt on the 18th?

We believe questions are the answer.

Learn to ask better questions and a lot of the mental game will fall into place. You will have a system you can stick with through thick and thin. A system that is not dependent on holing the putt. It is a system you get to have 100 per cent control over IF you choose that path.

The great coach Fred Shoemaker who has had such a big influence on our thinking said many years ago: "One of the bravest things a golfer can stay open to is the possible."

So with that in mind, perhaps the foundation of great putting is the question: "Is it possible that I could hole this putt?"

Is it? The answer of course is yes. Unless you choose otherwise.

Is it possible you could hit a drive 400 yards? Probably not!

You will have done the 'walk' focusing on your body as you move towards the green to give yourself a present moment awareness but then as you get onto the surface you could ask a very good question: "Is it possible that I could hole this putt?"

You could try to make statements like 'I am going to hole this' which has a win/lose closed-loop scenario that tends to go nowhere other than down. Or you could choose to ask the question: "Is it possible that I could hole this putt?"

Again, it is your choice as to how you answer this question but it is surely possible.

The very fact that you believe it is possible now has your mind open to that possibility. You are not bound by a past story. You may well have holed nothing all day, you may well have struggled with the putter, it may be the 15th hole and nothing has gone in but you can still choose to ask the question: "Is it possible that I could hole this putt?"

And, again, the answer is yours to choose. The bravest thing you can do is stay open to the possible.

You start with your first possible as you walk onto the 1st green and you only run out of possible on the 18th hole. Unless you choose to stop asking the question earlier in the round, if you choose to close your mind to possibility, and then you shut down the opportunity.

There is a whole world of difference between making a statement you have no control over and asking a question that puts you in a position of control.

You cannot control if the ball finds its way into the hole but you can stay open to that possibility.

We have found this liberates a player from the endless loop of insanity of trying to be positive but then giving up to being negative.

It creates a wonderfully calm kind of neutral state that just gets immersed in the task at hand, which is to roll this ball here – in this unique moment in time – towards that hole over there.

This unique putt that you have never had before and will never have again.

The 'possible' question is a grounding force – it keeps you away from negative stories and false promises. It returns you back to the simple task of rolling a ball. It is a wonderfully liberating way to play the game. Rather than the rollercoaster of trying to be positive and then falling into the trap of negativity, possible keeps you in a neutral space that gives you the foundation to allow putts to find the hole.

You are not in a constant battle with your mind.

It is from this standpoint that real consistency can emerge. Everyone tends to think that a 'routine' is a series of physical steps you take to get ready for a putt, when in fact what we have discovered is that it is far more important what kind of mental routine you have.

Answering the 'possible' question then gives you the opportunity to ask the second and perhaps even more important question to give you the best chance with the putt you are facing.

You will have walked onto the green created a neutral and open state of mind and then gathered the information suggested elsewhere in this book. As you look from behind the ball, what do you imagine could be the single most important question to ask yourself?

A question that will have you absorbed in the task at hand.

Very much aligned to what you have to do here and now as opposed to what the putt may or may not be for. It is so simple, yet so profoundly effective.

What does this ball need to do to go in the hole? Again: What does this ball need to do to go in the hole?

That is it. The million-dollar question. What does this ball need to do to go in the hole?

Given our understanding that once we pose a question to our mind it will go in search of the answer.

To answer the question "what does this ball need to do to go in the hole?" our mind will 'go to work'.

It will start to create a line, it will sense a pace.

It will come up with an answer. Will the answer always be the correct one? Perhaps, perhaps not.

But the more you ask this question, the more the habit develops and the more you will find your powerful supercomputer between your ears will start to come up with some good answers.

You may notice that after you have answered the question an image forms in your mind.

The image formed will be different for everyone.

The absolute key is to ask the question but more importantly WAIT for the answer. At times the answer will come instantly to you. At other times the answer will take a little longer to form in your mind but, for sure, if you ask the question you WILL start to answer it.

The answer to the question is a map that gives your body a direction to follow.

It seems so ridiculously simple to be almost absurd, but we have found that so many golfers get so lost in trying to make a perfect stroke that they lose sight of the ultimate objective which is to roll the ball on a desired line at a desired pace to a target.

When we are more concerned with the how of the putting stroke we leave our brain body connection floundering as to what it is supposed to do.

Is it supposed to make a 'good' stroke or is it supposed to roll the ball into the hole?

You may say that a good stroke will roll it into the hole. Yes, a good stroke is better than a poor one but a great stroke with a lack of clear intent will never be effective. You will never use the stroke for its real purpose.

We have seen some great putters with some very dodgy strokes but what they do have is crystal-clear intent. They know what they want that ball to do and their body organises the motion around that intent. With the answer to the question forming in your mind you will experience what we believe to be a game changing principle. The putt creates the stroke not the other way around.

Your next putt has no past and no future

The great thing about these questions is that no matter what has happened before or what may or may not happen in the future you can choose to ask these questions. This is something you can have total ownership of.

The ability to ask these questions keeps you grounded in what is going on right here and now. We hear so much about 'staying in the moment' but very little advice as to how to go about doing that. How do we get there? Questions actually provide the framework for being present to your experience.

The question 'what does this ball have to do to go in the hole?' allows you to 'create' a putt.

We firmly believe that the biggest breakthrough you will have is when you let go of the notion of just mindlessly repeating a stroke over and over within two rails or within a gadget and you embrace the idea that each putt is a unique moment in time, a moment you have never had before and a moment you will never have again.

Yes, practising your stroke can give you the skills to handle the requirement of the task but what if you believed that when you ask the question and, more importantly, when you answer the question you will create the images your body can organise around?

Your body will organise an appropriate movement in this unique moment. You have the resources to do that. Just imagine how liberating that concept is.

You may have missed some putts on previous greens but that is irrelevant. This putt is another brand-new opportunity.

How would it be if you embraced the idea that this particular putt you have in front of you has no past and no future?

This task here in front of you is a unique opportunity to 'create' a putt in this once-in-a-lifetime moment.

All of a sudden you get to create a new putt and in creating a new putt you are embracing a new story, a new way to act on the greens. When you let go of the idea of trying to recreate the stroke you had yesterday then you create a strange but wonderful liberation.

If, today, you are trying to 'recreate' what you had yesterday and today it doesn't feel anything like yesterday then you are stuck. You are stuck trying to 'find' something that has gone.

If, however, you embrace what you have today, even if it doesn't feel great, then you get the opportunity to create this putt in this moment.

How many times have you hit a putt with what feels like an awful stroke and it goes in?

By the same token, how many times have you hit a putt with what feels like the purest stroke ever and the ball somehow misses?

We have all had that experience. When we let go of the notion that the stroke needs to 'feel' right to hole putts we can go with what we have today.

The irony is that when you embrace what you have today and you get completely absorbed in the task here in front of you it is so strange how the body manages to get the job done if the intention is clear.

When you have a clear intent to what you want this putt to do in this moment and you trust your body to organise it, what can happen is fascinating.

If, however, the stroke feels poor and you get distracted by trying to fix it out on the course then your intention is weakened.

It is as if your brain doesn't know what you really want it to do: hole the putt or make a perfect stroke?

Having a crystal-clear intention is so very powerful and the way to have clear intent is to ask the question 'what does this ball have to do to go in the hole?'. Wait for the answer and as the answer emerges your intention becomes clear.

Your brain and body are aligned and they can go to work on making your intention a reality.

You will be able to maintain your attention in a useful place, namely that of getting the ball to interact with the hole and gravity.

We are not suggesting you shouldn't do any work on your stroke, far from it. There is plenty of good information out there to cater for that.

What we are saying is that, when you play, you need to have the discipline to go with what you have that day and not get distracted by how your stroke feels.

This will take a leap of faith and a change from what you have probably done for years.

However, as we have said all along, if the approach you currently are using was working you probably wouldn't be reading this book.

Your story will stay the same unless you change the way you approach your putting and in particular what you put your precious attention on. Understanding the value and effect of these two simple questions can be the foundation of a totally new and far more exciting story in the future.

1 Is it possible for the ball to go in the hole?
2 What does the ball need to do to go in the hole?

This is not a biblical text but clearly many years ago some wise folk had an inkling of the power of questions when they said: 'Ask and ye shall receive.'

Ask these two questions before each and every putt you are about to create and you will open up a whole new world of what is possible.

Key takeaways

1 We cannot stop ourselves from asking and answering questions. In the main, golfers ask dreadful questions. Poor questions assist poor attention and poor attention will help you to miss a whole bunch of putts.

2 Question One is perhaps the foundation of great putting: Is it possible that I could hole this putt? The answer of course is yes. Unless you choose otherwise.

3 Question Two: What does this ball need to do to go in the hole?

4 So many golfers get so lost in trying to make a perfect stroke that they lose sight of the ultimate objective which is to roll the ball on a desired line at a desired pace to a target.

5 Embrace the idea that each putt is a unique moment in time, a moment you have never had before and a moment you will never have again. Every putt is another brand-new opportunity.

6 Having a crystal-clear intention is powerful and the way to get it is to ask the question: "What does this ball have to do to go in the hole?" Wait for the answer and as the answer emerges your intention becomes clear.

THE TRUTH ABOUT PUTTING DATA

With Chris Sells, founder of strokeaverage.com

WITHOUT question, golf is more than a physical game. It is also an emotional one. Golfers often remember the highlights and lowlights – and this is also something that we see when watching TV coverage.

We are on the golf course for a long time –anywhere between three and five hours – but the time spent actually in the process of hitting shots is considerably shorter.

Many times, we hear people telling stories about their round in the 19th hole of what they did on certain shots but few are commenting on the ordinary golf shots.

They tell you what they did poorly or what they did that was beyond their expectations. They are naturally focusing on what they feel emotionally are the shots you will be interested in. The same can be said of the people who are controlling the TV coverage.

As a result of these emotional influences, we tend to have distorted opinions of what others do and, more frequently, what the pros do.

The only way really to see and properly understand what has actually happened is to study the individual shot data for a given player's overall round or to walk round and follow an individual group for the round's entire duration.

Nowadays, the best publicly available data is on the PGA Tour via their ShotLink system.

Over a decade, they have worked out the average putt conversions from various putting distances:. We can also have a closer look at some of the all-time records.

PGA Tour putt-conversion percentages

DISTANCE IN FEET	CONVERSION PERCENTAGE
1	100%
2	99%
3	95%
4	86%
5	75%
6	65%
7	56%
8	49%
9	43%
10	38%
12	30%
15	22%
20	14%
25	10%
30	7%
35	5%
40	4%
50	3%
60	2%
75	1%
90	0.50%

PGA Tour records: Fewest Putts Per Round

Eight players have recorded just 18 putts in a single round:

YEAR AND EVENT	ROUND	PLAYER
1979 IVB Philadelphia Classic	Final Round	Sam Trahan
1987 Fedex St Jude Classic	1st Round	Mike McGee
1989 MCI Heritage Classic	1st Round	Kenny Knox
1990 Anheuser-Busch Golf Classic	2nd Round	Andy North
1992 Fedex St Jude Classic	2nd Round	Jim McGovern
2000 Bell Canadian Open	2nd Round	Corey Pavin
2009 WGC CA Championship	3rd Round	Ken Duke
2010 Verizon Heritage	2nd Round	Blake Adams

How did they do it? ShotlLink Data only exists for these two. The total footage holed is similar in each case. Each holed from off the green four times. Their average holed putt per hole? Ken Duke 3ft 1in (43ft /14 holes); Blake Adams 3ft 2in (44ft 2in/14).

	KEN DUKE			BLAKE ADAMS		
Conventional Long Game Stats	Fairways Hit 9/14			Fairways Hit 10/14		
	Driving Distance All Drives 275			Driving Distance All Drives 255		
	Greens in Regulation 7/18			Greens in Regulation 8/18		
Recorded Putt Lengths	Attempts	Holed	Conversion %	Attempts	Holed	Conversion %
<3ft	7	7	100%	10	10	100%
3-5ft	6	6	100%	2	2	100%
5-7ft	1	1	100%	0		N/A
7-10ft	2	0	0	1	1	100%
10-15ft	1	0	0	1	1	100%
15-20ft	0		N/A	1	0	0%
20-25ft	0		N/A	1	0	0%
>25ft	1		0	2	0	0%
Shots holed from off the green		4			4	
Longest Putt Holed		6' 5"			14' 2"	
Total Holed Footage		43' 0"			44' 2"	

PGA Tour records: Fewest Putts at a 72-hole Strokeplay tournament

YEAR AND EVENT	PLAYER	TOTAL PUTTS FOR THE 4 ROUND TOURNAMENT
2005 MCI Heritage	David Frost	92
1989 MCI Heritage Classic	Kenny Knox	93
2002 Greater Greensboro Chrysler Classic	Mark Calcavecchia	93
2013 WGC Cadillac Championship	Brian Gay	93

So how did they do it? ShotLink Data is available for two of them:

	DAVID FROST			BRIAN GAY		
Conventional Long Game Stats	Fairways Hit 32/56			Fairways Hit 30/56		
	Driving Distance All Drives 258			Driving Distance All Drives 267		
	Greens in Regulation 25/72			Greens in Regulation 29/72		
Recorded Putt Lengths	Attempts	Holed	Conversion %	Attempts	Holed	Conversion %
<3ft	32	32	100%	34	34	100%
3-5ft	15	15	100%	15	14	93.33%
5-7ft	10	8	80.00%	9	5	55.56%
7-10ft	7	5	71.43%	7	6	85.71%
10-15ft	10	6	60.00%	16	9	56.25%
15-20ft	7	1	14.29%	2	1	50.00%
20-25ft	3	2	66.67%	5	0	0
>25ft	8	1	12.50%	5	1	20.00%
Shots holed from off the green		2			2	
Longest Putt Holed		27' 10"			41' 3"	
Total Holed Footage for 4 rounds		367' 11"			349' 4"	

PGA Tour records: Highest footage of holed putts during a season

YEAR	PLAYER	RNDS	AVG	TOTAL DIST (INCHES)	TOTAL RNDS	AVG DIST	BEST RND
2017	Peter Malnati	91	79'0"	69,222	73	4'6"	211'0"
2017	Ben Martin	86	72'6"	60,932	70	4'1"	210'1"
2016	Rickie Fowler	80	69'5"	53,325	64	3'11"	215'0"
2015	Sergio Garcia	59	75'5"	32,596	36	4'3"	220'5"
2014	Chris Stroud	88	75'6"	65,246	72	4'3"	221'4"
2013	D.H. Lee	65	74'0"	51,530	58	4'2"	201'6"
2013	Jin Park	52	70'7"	36,402	43	3'11"	209'5"
2011	Hunter Mahan	92	81'4"	74,161	76	4'7"	220'2"
2011	Johnson Wagner	81	80'11"	67,980	70	4'6"	202'9"
2011	Zack Miller	86	75'0"	67,489	75	4'3"	211'10"
2011	Nathan Green	81	72'1"	60,542	70	4'1"	219'0"
2011	Josh Teater	104	71'10"	79,300	92	4'0"	210'4"

	CHRIS STROUD 2014 CROWNE PLAZA INVITATIONAL AT COLONIAL 24 PUTTS		
Conventional Long Game Stats	Fairways Hit 8/14 Driving Distance All Drives 271 Greens in Regulation 13/18		
Distance	Attempts	Holed	Conversion %
<3ft	5	5	100%
3-5ft	4	4	100%
5-7ft	2	2	100%
7-10ft	2	1	50.00%
10-15ft	2	0	0.00%
15-20ft	2	1	50.00%
20-25ft	2	2	100%
>25ft	5	3	60.00%
Shots holed from off the green		None	
Longest Putt Holed		56' 4"	
Total Holed Footage		221' 4"	

Our thoughts on this data

What Chris's fascinating data just goes to show is that once outside seven feet even the very best putters on the planet miss more than they hole. This is not a negative – it is just a statistical reality. It gives you the opportunity to be just that little bit kinder to yourself when you miss. It also allows a more even and realistic perspective on the game so you can move on to the next opportunity. Watching golf on TV can be very misleading as the action will keep cutting to a player holing a putt, giving the impression that 20 footers are going in all of the time. The statistics say otherwise.

As we will keep saying, our Putting Performance Principles give you the best possible chance to hole more putts but within that premise you also need to build in the mental resilience to deal with a lot of putts that you may hit very well but just don't go in the hole. As long as you have gone through your process, you have done your part. Once you own your process, you can deal with the putts that do miss so much better.

At the other end of the scale though, the fact that eight players on the PGA Tour have completed a round with only 18 putts does give a hint of what could be possible if you are absorbed in the task of rolling the ball at the appropriate pace on the appropriate line into this hole at this unique moment in time.

• **StrokeAverage.com** is the brainchild of founder Chris Sells. Chris started working as the official golf analyst for the English Golf Union in 2001 and conceived the StrokeAverage.com approach. Chris was an integral part of Paul McGinley's winning Ryder Cup team, providing data analysis before and during the event. He works with several tour players and coaches including Peter Cowen and David Leadbetter. Unique in its depth, flexibility, and ease of use, StrokeAverage.com is designed for players and coaches of all standards. Free two-week trials available at **chrissellsgolf.com** and **strokeaverage.com**

Chapter 4
LINE & PACE

WE have another very important question for you. In your opinion, what is the most important factor in putting, line or pace?

This is one of the first questions we ask any golfer when working with them to improve their putting. Whether that person is a weekend golfer, a seasoned professional or winner of major championships, this question is equally valid.

Why? Quite simply because in order to help any golfer become a better putter, we first need to understand their perception of how they intend to get the ball in the hole and subsequently, what is their INTENTION and where they are placing their ATTENTION.

More often than not, their initial response to this vital question is line, always line, definitely line. Line is everything. We then ask why they prioritise line over pace. The most common answers include:

"Well, if it's on line, it always has a chance of going in."

"The ball can't go in if it's not on the right line."

"Now that I come to think of it, I'm actually pretty good at getting the line right, but my pace isn't always great."

That is generally the moment when the penny drops. The moment when they realise that while they may be placing more importance or value on line, in actual fact, the reason they don't hole more putts is pretty straight forward. They aren't getting the pace right.

After a bit of thought, deliberation and a short discussion, 100 per cent of the people we work with then decide – we don't tell them, they draw their own conclusions – that pace is in fact more important than line.

So, once we have determined that if we are going to prioritise one aspect over the other, pace leapfrogs line and becomes the number one priority. PACE IS KEY AND PACE IS KING, PACE GIVES YOU OPTIONS.

Pace determines line. In fact we'd go so far as to say that without pace, the line does not or cannot exist.

Over and above that, there has been a lot of research done on how the effective size of the hole changes relative to the pace the ball is travelling.

"The speed of the putt dictates the size of the hole. The size of the hole being 4.25 inches. One revolution of the ball is 5.26 inches long, about the length of a dollar bill (or £10 note). Each revolution shrinks the effective width of the hole by 12 per cent.

The harder you hit a putt, the smaller the hole gets and the less the chance you have of making the putt."
– Former PGA Tour pro Darrell Kestner

If your ball has enough speed to travel:
6 inches past – the hole width is 3.8 inches
12 inches past – the hole width is 2.6 inches
24 inches past – the hole width is 1.9 inches
36 inches past – the hole width is 1.4 inches

The graphic overleaf gives us a stronger visual impression of what this means in practice.

Dead weight, middle of
the hole = 4.25" hole width.

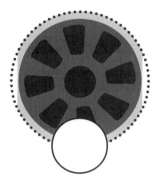

6" Past = 3.8" hole width

1 foot past = 2.6" hole width

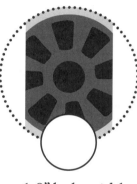

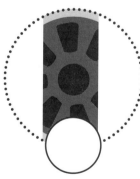

2 feet past = 1.9" hole width

3 feet past = 1.4" hole width

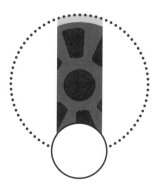

What Darrell doesn't mention is that a putt travelling at dead weight and finishing in the middle of the hole makes the hole its entire 4.25 inches wide.

As the hole is obviously circular, this means that it is also 4.25 inches from front to back. How many times have you hit a "great putt" that has come up an inch short bang on line? Probably two or three times in every round of golf you have ever played.

What would have happened if your intended target had been the back of the hole and not the front and your ball had come up an inch short of that target? It would have gone right in the middle!

In order for the ball to go in the hole, it has to have a relationship with momentum and gravity. If the ball is traveling with too much momentum, then gravity cannot take its effect. Too little momentum and the ball won't reach the hole. Pretty straightforward really.

We're sure you agree that this presents a pretty strong case for paying particular ATTENTION to pace.

We are not advocating that line isn't important – of course it is.

We are, however, saying that the correct line on any given putt is directly influenced by the correct pace.

And when a player focuses more on pace they free up their stroke and their natural ability to hit the putt on line improves dramatically.

If pace determines line, what determines pace? There are a number of factors that play a part including the contours and speed of the greens.

Is your putt uphill or downhill? Have the greens just been cut? Are you putting into the wind or is the wind helping? Is the wind from your left or from your right? Yes, the wind can actually affect your putts.

The concept of pace determining line

We will delve deeper into how you can actually start to read and figure out pace later in the green-reading section but, for now, let's keep our attention on the concept of pace determining the line. Perhaps for the first time, you will experience a genuine shift in your concept of putting.

Since the late 1980s, we have both had amazing opportunities to observe, work with and learn from some of the best putters in world golf.

While we don't believe that there is a long list of technical musts that create excellent putters, there are some commonalities that allow great putters to perform at an exceptional level.

In no particular order, these commonalities are: they all do it their own way; they are very aware of where their attention needs to be; they all strongly believe in what they are doing; and they all have excellent distance control or pace.

They all work hard at finding the best way to get their golf ball to do what they want it to.

They may well have been influenced by great putters they have played with or admired or taken advice from coaches they trusted but ultimately they all worked towards becoming the best version of themselves that they possibly could.

One of the main things that inspired us to write this book is that, while we understand pace has more value than line, the majority of coaching, instruction and training aids, devices and gadgets tend to focus on or obsess about two things.

What we as golfers need to do with our body and with our putter.

Aim and start line. We have to get the start line right. We must get the ball starting on line.

We're not saying this is wrong. Well, not entirely anyway.

Yes, you still need to be aware of where the putter is aiming at address and facing at the point of contact. Good alignment is an essential aspect of becoming a great putter.

We are merely suggesting that if you have read all the instruction articles and manuals, tried all of these training aids, watched all of the video tutorials and you still don't putt as well as you think or believe you can, let's look at putting slightly differently, let's open our minds to a different concept.

You'll be amazed that by focusing on pace, your brain and body will organise what they need to do to get the start line better anyway.

This is one of those anomalies where you get better at something by NOT focusing on it. Strange but true.

We have all read the books, seen the videos, used the technology and tried the training aids and gadgets.

They all focus on one end of the putt: the start; the end where we are focusing on our putter, trying out yet another gadget, a thinner grip, a thicker grip, a different way of holding the putter – and that's before we even get to our numerous "stroke thoughts".

However, as you will have gleaned from Chapter 3, we believe you need to pay more attention to the other end of the putt. The part where the hole is. After all, that's where we want the ball to go. Our intention is ultimately to get the ball to go in the hole. No one ever asked: "How many putting strokes did you have today?"

We have searched long and hard for a scorecard that has a box for the number of putting strokes you had without success – they don't exist and we're really not interested in that. We are, however, very interested in how many putts you had.

Gary remembers being introduced to the concept that pace was more important than line at a very early stage in his golfing life when his late father suggested he concentrate a bit more on trying to get the distance better with his putts after three-putting for the fourth time one Sunday morning.

The frustrating three-putts were due almost entirely to hitting his first putts four feet past or leaving them six feet short.

He was only 10 years old at the time and while he didn't really understand the concept of pace determining the line, he did stop three- putting as frequently!

His earliest recollection of pace being mentioned by a professional golfer was when he caddied for a friend of his at the time, Andrew

Oldcorn whom he later went on to coach for over 10 years, at the Open Championship at Turnberry in 1986.

"Greg Norman won and we didn't – but that's beside the point!

"We were on the 1st green on a windy Thursday morning, facing a slippery, downhill left to right five footer to save par when all my fears were realised. He wanted my opinion on the line. I wasn't ready for that!

"Naively, I thought I was only there to carry the bag and take the blame for a missed green or fairway. That still happened but I wasn't expecting to have to read greens as well.

"On to the green I went in my pristine white boiler suit – compulsory attire for caddies at the Open back then – and asked what his opinion was before I dare offer mine. What a smart move that turned out to be.

"'Downhill, left to right,' he replied.

"I agreed wholeheartedly, although how much left to right was never discussed. 'It's all about the pace,' I was told before being dispatched to the side of the green.

"As I stood watching the ball start rolling, I remember quite clearly thinking 'I didn't see that much break' before the ball slowly disappeared into the hole at the perfect pace.

"What did I learn from that? He saw the pace and therefore the line differently to me. From that moment on, whenever I was asked to look at or confirm a line, I always made a point of saying that it was 'all about the pace'."

Throughout his career, Oldcorn has been a good putter and, at times, a great putter. Namely when he won three tournaments on the European Tour including the 2001 PGA Championship at Wentworth, holding off Nick Faldo and Angel Cabrera down the stretch. His putting prowess was largely down to his understanding of pace and his ability to consistently strike the ball out the sweet spot of whatever putter he used (and he's used a few!) in order to get the ball rolling at the desired pace.

You'll note that we mentioned hitting the ball out the sweet spot in the previous paragraph. This is vitally important if you are to have any chance of hitting your putts the correct distance.

Most modern putters have a built-in alignment aid in one form or another but most golfers we see tend to use them for ensuring the putting is "square" to their intended target or start line.

Nothing wrong with that whatsoever but that alignment aid should also be used to make sure we have the middle of the putter and the middle of the ball match up in order to give you the greatest chance of hitting the ball the correct distance – or basically getting the pace right.

We know that if we hit our driver out the heel or toe, the resultant shots rarely travel the full or desired distance or direction. The same applies to an off-centre strike with your putter.

That is not our personal opinion: we have done a lot of testing and research to reach this conclusion.

In fact, a heel or toe strike on a 10-foot putt can result in the ball traveling less than 80 per cent of the intended distance.

We all know we should strike the ball out the sweet spot but when was the last time you actually paid any ATTENTION to doing just that? Something worth looking at? We certainly believe so.

From what we have witnessed as coaches over the years, the majority of golfers tend to address the ball slightly toe-side of centre. As a result, the majority of their putts come up short. Did they make bad strokes? Generally not. Did they mis-strike them or miss the sweet spot? Generally yes.

"When I have putted my best, before a tournament round I always paid attention to hitting the ball out the sweet spot. Not really thinking about holing putts, just focusing on a centred strike. That made it so much easier to see and feel the pace because I knew how the ball was going to react to a centred strike. I viewed putts like full shots, I was focusing on getting the ball to go where I wanted it to and I knew that the better the strike was, the better my chances were of holing putts on the golf course."
– *Gordon Brand Jnr, two-time Ryder Cup player, winner of eight European Tour events and two European Seniors Tour events.*

Some factual information based on our research

In the process of writing this book, we conducted an awful lot of research and in our quest to provide you with the best information possible, we have studied research from some highly respected experts. Mark Broadie, whose incredibly detailed and well researched book Every Shot Counts contains some very interesting insights that might surprise you.

• On the PGA Tour, on average, pros leave almost exactly 50 per cent of 30-foot putts short. They leave seven per cent of 10-foot putts short on average, with the best putters leaving only six per cent short and the worst leaving nine per cent short.

Whereas amateur golfers who shoot in the 90s tend to leave 16 per cent of similar length putts short.

Amateur golfers also miss 70 per cent of their putts on the low side. The most important distance for 'strokes gained' on the PGA Tour is five feet, whereas for amateurs the most important distance is four feet. Based on this research, we think you will agree that pace is unquestionably a key component to becoming a great putter.

Don't believe us? Here's Jordan Spieth, winner of three majors, the Masters, US Open and the Open Championship, by the age of 24: "The best tip I've ever had is tough to narrow down but I always remember Ben Crenshaw telling me how crucial it is to work on my speed on the greens.

"Putting with him was very special and he stressed not to worry about my stroke but focus on the speed. That's good advice. If you hit your putts with the right pace, somewhere near the right line, you're going to scare the hole.

"When my pace feels good, when I start to get really dialled in, that's when the putts start to go in."

Earlier we mentioned the majority of putting coaching, training aids and technology tend to focus largely on what we need to do with ourselves and our putter and the start line of the putt.

Again, we're not saying this is wrong. There have been lots of very good putters who have focused their attention at this end of the putt but ultimately, to hole more putts, we need to pay more attention to what the ball needs to do to go in the hole.

Early in 2017, we were asked to trial the latest TrackMan Performance Putting software.

We've all seen TrackMan on TV coverage and the golf industry recognises them as the market leaders in capturing ball and club data on full shots, especially the big booming drives we see in the world of professional golf. For TrackMan to develop a programme devoted entirely to putting was a welcome addition for us – and indeed the golf coaching world – in our quest to help our students hole more putts.

At last, here was something that would accurately measure exactly what the ball does during any given putt.

There is some great technology out there for measuring what the putter does during the execution of a putt but nothing as far as we are aware that measures the entirety of a putt quite like TrackMan.

The SAM (Science And Motion) Putt Lab is a fantastic piece of technology which is great for measuring face at aim, face at impact, path of the stoke, strike point, dynamic loft, tempo – the list goes on – and we find it an excellent tool for coaching and fitting.

However, it doesn't provide any ball data. That may change in the future but at the time of writing, it only provides club data. Excellent club data, we hasten to add.

During a visit to TrackMan HQ in Denmark in 2017 to attend their inaugural Leadership and Innovation Forum, we learned a great deal about their new and exciting putting software.

Initially they chose to launch V1 providing only ball data with fantastic clubhead data since being released in V2.

This created a very interesting debate among the good people at Trackman and the other attendees, golf coaches and club fitters, invited from around the world.

After much discussion, it was agreed that ball data only would be the way forward initially.

Why? Because no one else was tracking and measuring what the ball does for the entirety of the putt and we all agreed it would be enormously helpful to learn about how the ball reacts when struck by a putter.

If we can measure how the ball reacts, surely that has to be helpful in our quest to hole more putts, shoot lower scores and have more fun.

Since then, we have done a lot of research and experimentation with TrackMan Putting Performance software to see how a change of focused attention alters the distance or pace of putts.

It is not our opinion that results change, we are using highly accurate measured data. As our good friends at TrackMan always say: "Why guess what you can measure?"

By focusing on what the ball needs to do to go in the hole, as you will now know from asking our two questions (see Chapter 3) there are numerous benefits to be found from this simple but highly effective concept.

The creative people in the tech department at TrackMan are an exceptionally smart and innovative bunch and for them to agree with us that we should start paying more focused attention to what the ball does, or indeed needs to do, to go in the hole, was a sign that we were quite literally on the right track.

With that in mind, rather than trying to create a perfect stroke, whatever that looks like, we'd like you to focus on the concept of creating a putt.

Creating a putt

Instinctively, if we asked you to roll a ball to the hole or the edge of a putting green like a crown-green bowler, where would your attention be? How far you take your hand or arm back? Was that too far on the inside? How much wrist break you would or wouldn't use? How far would you follow through?

When we ask our students, the answers to these questions is a resounding NO.

So if we aren't focusing on what we need to do with various parts of our body in order to roll the ball the correct distance and direction, what are we focusing on?

The answer is of course pace.

You might be surprised at just how good you are at this. Don't underestimate your instincts – after all they've probably served you pretty well in your daily life so far.

We have all experienced that feeling when we walk onto a green, mark our ball, have a look at what we need to do to get the ball in the hole and think: "I'm going to hole this."

Why is that? Essentially because, in our mind's eye, we have seen the ball travelling on the correct line at the correct pace with crystal-clear clarity. We talk about visualisation in Chapter 6 but think about this in the meantime.

Jack Nicklaus once said: "I never hit a bad shot or a bad putt in my mind before I hit it." Basically, he was saying he never saw a shot miss the fairway, miss the green or not go in the hole in his mind's eye.

That may be mis-interpreted purely as "positive thinking" or having a "positive mental attitude" but what he was really saying was that he had fantastic clarity of what the ball needed to do in order to reach his intended target.

At no point did he say 'I never made a bad swing or a bad putting stroke in my mind'.

He wasn't trying to create swings or putting strokes, he was creating shots and putts. There is a whole world of difference between these two concepts.

You will have noticed by now that one of our favourite words is attention and the more you read this book and apply the Putting Performance Principles covered in it, you will start to truly understand that golf is a game of attention.

When you are on the practice green working on your putting, chances are there won't be too many distractions. Therefore, you can pay particular attention to what the ball needs to do to go in the hole, once you have ascertained that it is in fact possible for that to happen.

You won't be thinking about the three-putt you had on the 3rd green last Sunday, the short one you missed on the last to lose a fiver, or that one of your playing partners is so painfully slow that he might actually take root if he stands over his putt any longer.

Find a quiet spot on the practice green and work on getting your pace right.

Try this from a variety of distances. Long ones, short ones, left-to-right breaking putts, right-to-left breaking putts, uphill, downhill, try to cover them all.

You'll soon discover that when you get the pace right, your second putts, if you don't hole the first one, will more often than not be tap-ins.

Take a notebook with you and record your results. We're not asking you to write down exactly where every single putt finishes but at the end of the session, make notes on where the majority of your putts finish. Are they long, short, left, right or in the hole?

If you do this every time you work on creating putts, you will soon start to see patterns forming.

These patterns show up facts, not opinions. Opinions tend to lead to emotional reactions which are rarely helpful, so let's stick to dealing with the facts.

They will help to direct you to what you really need to focus on.

That could well be pace.

It could be that most of the putts you hole are right-to-left uphill putts from inside six feet.

It might be that the majority of your left-to-right downhill putts from between 10 and 15 feet finish short and right of the hole due to insufficient pace.

Whatever your findings, they will definitely help you on your journey to becoming a far better creator of putts.

You may well be thinking 'I'm not a very creative type, so I'm going to struggle with creating anything, never mind a putt that goes in the hole'.

Not true. Every time you have finished a golf hole, you have done just that.

You may have taken more shots than you would have liked to

finish the hole but at some point during every hole in every round of golf you have ever played or every practice putting session you have ever had, you will have created a putt that goes in the hole.

The Zone

Take some time to sit back and reflect on some of the memorable putts you have holed in the past.

Think back to where you were, not just physically but mentally. What was your intention and where was your attention? Chances are you were in the present. The here and now. The task at hand. The 'zone'. Where is this mythical place they call "the zone"? You won't find it hiding in the sat nav in your car nor will you find it with a search on Google maps.

It does exist but there is no postcode for it. It exists in your mind. It exists when you have complete clarity of what needs to happen for the ball to go in the hole.

When you can rid your mind of the useless, unhelpful clutter that distracts you from the simple task in hand.

Essentially it exists when you become extremely calm once you have asked yourself and answered the two questions from Chapter 3.

Almost everyone who has ever played golf has experienced this at some point in their golfing life, albeit largely fleetingly.

One of the main purposes of this book is to provide you with some concepts and principles to help you achieve that calm state of mind if not on demand, certainly on a more regular basis.

'Calm state of mind' - wouldn't that be a nice place to be when standing over a three foot putt, or any length of putt for that matter?

While there may not be a postcode you can type in to take you there, understanding and applying the Putting Performance Principles in this book will enable you to train your mind through these simple but highly effective processes to create that sense of calmness.

As you will have gathered by now, there is a direct correlation between line and pace and our two questions.

Opening up your mind to what is possible - Is it possible for the ball to go in the hole? – allows you to direct your focused attention on "what does the ball need to do to go in the hole?"

The answers to which are obviously a) yes and b) travel on the right line at the appropriate pace.

When we speak to players who have experienced great putting rounds, they rarely go into any kind of detail about how good their stroke felt. They might say "I putted beautifully" or "I felt I was going to hole everything I looked at today".

Tiger Woods often talks about when he was winning majors, his "lag" or pace putting was spot on.

He understood the importance of getting the pace of his putts bang on. Strangely enough, many other top tour pros did too.

Here's what Andrew Coltart, Sky Sports golf analyst, Ryder Cup player, two-time winner on both the PGA Tour of Australia and European Tour and winner of the Alfred Dunhill Cup at St Andrews with Sam Torrance and Colin Montgomerie has to say about putting.

"Putting was easy until I started overthinking it. As a child and junior, I would charge around the putting green with one ball holing putts for fun.

"It was the golf club's putting green and I knew the lines like the back of my hand but I could also feel the line of the putt under the soles of my feet. I spent days there just putting.

"In the early stages of my life on tour, I was a great putter. It was second nature. I saw the line and pace and then reacted almost immediately.

"There was a quiet thoughtlessness, yet certainty to what I was doing. I let the putt create the stroke and I never ever thought of the return putt!

"Of course, this all changed when I started copying other tour pros. Players whose games had reached a higher level but were by no means better putters. I started trying to emulate them, assuming they were doing it 'right' and, guess what, that's when it all started to go wrong.

"Putting with five or six balls. Why? You don't get a second chance on the golf course. Putting from 10 feet. Why? Statistics will tell you that you will miss more then you will hole from that range, so how can that be productive?

"When you look up, your brain registers the misses and not the holed putts. Putting mirrors – now I'm worrying about how my stroke looks and feels when really my attention should be on the hole and how my ball is going to get there. Standing over the ball too long trying to make a 'perfect' stroke. Your chances of doing that with a conscious thought diminish by the second.

"Nowadays, I would putt to a tee, so that I never see the ball not going in the hole. I would practice pace drills, because without the correct pace, the line is irrelevant.

"I would recommend spending more time holing out time after time from three feet. Listening to the ball drop and seeing it go in the hole, all very important.

"I would only ever putt with one ball – there are no second serves in golf – and try to make my practice as realistic and ultimately, as much fun as possible," he said.

What do you remember about the great putting days you have experienced?

Do you see your putting stroke in your imagination? Or, do you see the ball tracking towards, then disappearing into the hole on the perfect line at the perfect pace?

Without a doubt, one of the world's great putters is Jordan Spieth. It is incredible to see how many putts he holes from the six to 30-foot range.

He is unbelievable but if you watch his putts go in you will see his 'secret'. The ball seems to find the bottom of the cup time and time again because his pace control is so incredibly good.

You see a lot of his putts seem to be coming up short but they have just the right pace and the hole finds a way of grabbing the golf ball.

If you watch golf on TV, you may have noticed a "putt prediction system" graphic the broadcasters use.

They work closely with Hawk-Eye Innovations to illustrate that the line of a putt can vary massively according to the pace.

The visuals they create are fascinating and help bring the viewer closer to the action. We know the pros would love to see that graphic when they are standing over their putts!

Putt-View have created a similar Virtual Reality system which also predicts the line and pace to help you understand just how pace determines line. We'll talk more about them later in Chapter 6.

Six Exercises

We are not suggesting that you use all of these drills and exercises every time you go to the putting green but we would like you to try them all at some point.

Once you have tried them all, you'll soon figure out which ones give you the greatest feedback, results and enjoyment. Yes, we did say enjoyment. The golf industry in today's world is obsessed with distance, with all the manufacturers promising you additional yardage if you buy their latest clubs.

As a result, we are led to believe the only way we can enjoy our golf is if we hit the ball further. While that may well be true in some cases, not everyone will benefit from or be satisfied with a few extra yards. However, we can all increase our enjoyment levels of the game by shooting lower scores and having more fun on the golf course by simply putting a whole lot better. The following drills and exercises are designed to empower you to do just that. You will soon discover that holing putts is
extremely enjoyable and supremely satisfying.

Exercise 1: The deliberate miss

Set up with the ball in the middle of the sweet spot of your putter. No hole involved as this is purely a skill building exercise. Take five balls and make your stroke but deliberately hit the ball out of the toe of the putter. Notice how that feels.

Then take the same five balls one at a time setting up with the sweet spot but this time make your stroke and deliberately hit the ball out of the heel. Notice how that feels.

So, if you can hit it out of the toe on purpose and you can hit it out of the heel on purpose, what can you also do?

Exactly! Now take the five balls and 'trap' the feeling of hitting the ball out of the sweet spot. Really tune in to how it feels. How the ball rolls.

By experiencing what is 'wrong' your brain will be able to feel what is 'right'.

By heightening your senses this way and placing your attention on the point of contact on your putter your ability to judge pace will be very much improved.

Exercise: 2 Roll with it

This is quite possibly one of the simplest but most effective drills you could ever do. So simple you don't even need a putter!

The purpose of this drill is two-fold. Firstly, you will soon learn that instinctively you will understand the importance of what the ball needs to do. Secondly, it will give you a pretty good indication of the speed of the greens on any given day.

Take one golf ball and head to the putting green. Find a spot and roll the ball to the edge of the green. You might want to put a few tees in the ground where the green meets the fringe as a visual aid and roll your ball to the various tees.

Allow your brain and body to organise how much force you need to apply to perform this task. You'll be amazed how good you become at this in a very short space of time without the mental clutter of any kind of technical thoughts.

Exercise 3: Bradshaw's Balls

This is an exercise used by the late Harry Bradshaw, one of Ireland's greatest golfers who played in three Ryder Cups and won the Irish PGA Championship an astonishing 10 times.

Take two balls to the putting green. We know you normally take three and we actually advocate you should only take one (because we only get to putt with one ball on the golf course) but in this instance we need two. Putt your first ball to somewhere on the green but not to a hole. Pay close attention to how your ball reacts. Does it turn left to right? Does it gather speed as it goes over a little ridge on the green? How far did it travel?

With your second ball, try to imagine a spot under the first ball and dislodge that ball with enough pace so the second ball comes to rest on that very spot. If the second ball dislodges the first one and comes to rest where the first one originally lay, you will have hit your second putt on the right line with exactly the right pace.

Exercise 4: Pace only

This exercise takes a leap of faith but we have found with some players it can be an absolutely liberating experience. Go onto the putting green with just one ball and hit a bunch of RANDOM putts from all over the green ranging from 10ft to 30ft. What we want you to do differently is to just walk up to the ball and DO NOT read the line. Just look at the putt in terms of pace and your goal is to get the pace dead right. Just the pace! What we find with many players who do this exercise is that they get REALLY good at pace but the ultimate paradox is that the line also tends to be VERY good. Almost as if our on board super computer the unconscious mind does the job for you.

Exercise 5: Ladder To Success

This is one of our favourite drills – you can spend hours having fun with it. Set up a semi-circle of tees around and beyond the hole, a grip's length from the outside edge of the hole. Now put tees in the ground at one, two, three and four paces short of the hole.

Hit a putt from level with the tee at one pace away. Your aim is obviously to hole it but we're going to cut you some slack here as this is more about pace than anything. If your putt doesn't go in but does finish within the semi-circle of tees, you are allowed to move on to the next rung on the ladder. If you don't hole the putt and your ball finishes outside the semi-circle, start again from the same spot and try again until you achieve your goal.

Hit a putt from two paces from the hole. Again, your intention is to hole the putt or keep it within the semi-circle. Fail to do so, start again. Succeed and you move on to the next rung up the ladder.

Continue this process until you have either holed putts or kept them in the semi-circle from one, two, three and four paces. You can play around with this and make it tougher by not allowing yourself to move up the ladder until you have holed a putt from each distance. You don't have to stop at four paces. The best we have seen is 13 paces – think you can beat that?

Exercise 6: One-Armed Bandit

"Putting with one hand improves your ability to sink them with two," said Jackie Burke, winner of two major championships and five-time US Ryder Cup team member, who was recognised by his peers as an outstanding putter.

We all know that putting is all about feel and touch. We often hear TV commentators talk about how this player or that has "great feel on the greens" or "the touch of a Bond Street pickpocket".

Where does that feel come from? We've all been told to 'rock our shoulders and keep your hands out of it'.

Our counter to that would be: How much feel for direction or distance (line and pace) do you have with your shoulders? Do you have more touch or feel in your shoulders or in your hands? Take a couple of minutes to have a good think about that.

Take a ball to the putting green – remember, golf isn't like tennis and we don't get a second serve – and pick a hole three feet away.

If you are right-handed, see if you can hole it using your right hand only with your left hand behind your back or in your pocket.

If you are left-handed, use your left hand.

Chances are, whether you are right or left-handed, the one you use for just about everything on a daily basis is the hand that possesses more feel.

In order to create a putt that goes into the hole, we need to have a relationship with the tool we are using to make the ball do what we want it to. Using your "natural" hand will enable you to create and feel some kind of awareness of the direction your putter travels in and ultimately where it faces at the point of contact. If you allow your putter to become an extension of your natural hand, the chances are you will create an incredible awareness of what the putter is doing in a bid to control the essentials of line and pace.

Make sense?

Create a putt with your "natural" hand and roll the ball into the hole from three feet. You'll be surprised how quickly and easily you can achieve this without cluttering up your mind with technical thoughts. Try it from four feet. Still easy? Yes? Good.

Now try it from five feet then six feet. Try it from all sorts of distances using your natural hand to control the line and pace of your putts. If you're still not convinced, try the same exercise holding your putter in one hand then two hands controlling line and pace with your shoulders. We'd love to hear how you get on.

PUTTER DESIGN
With Sean Toulon and Austin Rollinson of Odyssey Golf

WE often talk to our students about forming a relationship with their putter and embarking on an incredible journey of discovery with it.

Statistics will tell you that you use your putter more than any other club in your bag. So it makes perfect sense to take some time in selecting the correct tool for the task at hand, namely holing putts.

We have all been in a pro shop and found ourselves drawn almost magnetically to the putter rack in search of The One that will cure all of our putting woes.

We pick one up, make a couple of practice strokes and say to ourselves 'that feels great' as we imagine holing putts from all over the place to win the monthly medal, the club championship or to take the money in the Sunday morning fourball before heading to the counter to purchase it.

However, do we ever take time to think of this latest acquisition as a precision tool designed to do a specific job? Is it the correct length? Does the design suit your particular stroke or style? Is the grip the correct thickness? Is the weight and balance going to help or hinder you in your quest?

We strongly recommend you take the time and effort to get your putter custom-fitted. Most golfers nowadays buy custom-fitted drivers, fairway woods, irons and even wedges but have you ever thought about having your putter custom-fitted? If not, we suggest you do.

Golf is a very individual sport and looking at the styles of all the greats who have putted their way to success over the years, the one thing they have in common is that they all do it their own way.

As putting is a very individual aspect of the game, it would appear pretty logical to ensure you are equipped with a putter that suits you and your particular style.

With that in mind, we asked our good friends at Odyssey for an insight into their design ethos in a bid to help you understand the importance of choosing the best putter for you.

A putting white paper

Sean Toulon, general manager of Odyssey Golf and a senior vice president of Callaway Golf, enlisted the help of his chief designer Austie Rollinson to put the following white paper together for your information and consideration.

Odyssey Golf have been creating and manufacturing the most innovative putters in golf since 1991. That's 27 years dedicated to advancing putter technology and design to help golfers on the greens. In that time, we've learned an enormous amount about putter performance by studying the physics of the putting stroke and the dynamics of impact. We've gained a deep understanding of the psychology behind what makes certain shapes and designs appealing and confidence-inducing. And we've developed in-depth knowledge of the myriad different putting styles employed by players of all abilities.

These learnings helped us identify six key focus areas we call the Odyssey Ethos: Shape; Alignment; Forgiveness; Sound; Feel; Roll.

These are the key zones in which we relentlessly pursue innovation, allowing us to develop the best-looking, best-performing putters in golf. The purpose of this white paper is to provide insight into our design philosophies in each of these six areas.

Shape

The head's shape is the first impression a golfer gets of a putter, so it's important that it be intriguing and appealing. We strive to devise shapes that are first and foremost unique, especially in our mallets. Our goal is to challenge the golfer's perception of what a putter should look like without ignoring tradition. In other words, we're ever-conscious of the fact that the shape can't be different to the point of being awkward or disagreeable in appearance. Establishing that balance between being unique and appealing is one of the putter designer's biggest challenges.

Our 2-Ball putter shape achieved this balance very successfully. During the design phase, we studied many different ways to position the two white discs on top. Early designs featured only 1 1/3 discs on a head shaped like our popular Rossie model. However, testing indicated this design didn't perform as well in terms of helping the golfer align the head accurately compared to larger heads with two full discs. In the end, we had to push ourselves into new design territory in pursuit of the best possible performance, leading us to balance a unique new crown design combining two discs with a familiar Rossie-type sole shape. That was the first 2-Ball, which went on to become one of the most successful and best-selling putter designs of all time.

Alignment

Our research indicates that face alignment at impact is extremely important to determining the line on which the ball leaves the face. That's crucial because we've found that as much as 90 per cent of a putt's direction is dictated by face orientation at impact. For example, on a straight, 10-foot putt, if your face angle is off by more than one degree, the ball will miss the hole. The path of the putter also affects the putt's direction, but only a fraction of the degree that face alignment does.

Features can be incorporated into the head to promote precise aiming. For a long time, such features were as simple as a small sight-line on the crown or back cavity.

More recently larger, bolder features have been applied. Mallet-style putters are ideal for designs that incorporate long and bold alignment features on the crown. For example, the 2-Ball putter's two ball-sized discs work with the ball at address to create a powerful alignment aid that easily shows precisely where the face is pointing. We've also used bold white or black lines stretching across the crown from the face to the back of the putter.

Golfers who have difficulty with alignment usually gravitate towards these kinds of putters, which is why we put a lot of effort in designing unique mallet designs with new and highly effective alignment aids.

Forgiveness

Many golfers have trouble consistently hitting putts with the centre of the face. That's a problem because impact away from the face's geometric centre, towards the toe or heel, causes the head to twist open or closed, affecting direction. It also causes inefficient energy transfer that can cause the putt to come up short.

To mitigate twisting on off-centre hits, we design features into our putters that increase the head's moment of inertia (MOI).

Accomplishing this calls for positioning mass as far away from the putter's centre of gravity (CG) as you can. The simplest way to do this is to increase the size of the footprint (the size of the putter as viewed from address). This is easiest to accomplish in a mallet, which is inherently bigger than a blade. A mallet's typically rounded shape is highly conducive to increasing size enough to dramatically raise MOI.

Putters can also be designed using multiple materials of different density to affect MOI. Using different materials makes it possible to create high-MOI designs that retain a smaller-sized footprint, which some golfers prefer.

Sound

The sound a putter makes at impact is important. The auditory feedback produced helps the golfer judge how hard to hit the putt. This perception helps build the golfer's confidence when he or she sees the ball roll out to the distance that meets his or her perceived expectation. Over time, a golfer becomes accustomed to this interplay between sound and distance. When the sound of impact fails to meet their distance expectation, doubt can creep in, and when it comes to putting, doubt is never good.

We spend a lot of time working on achieving the proper impact sound when we are designing our putters. However, we don't design the same exact sound into all of our models. We understand that different golfers have different expectations about the ideal sound in a putter. That's why we set up our putter lines to offer a variety of sounds from soft to very firm. This ensures that no matter what type of ball a golfer is using (which also affects sound), he or she can find an Odyssey putter that fits their taste in sound.

Experimentation and computer analysis helps ensure that each of our putter designs delivers the desired pitch and volume. Different sounds are achieved using several different methods, starting with face material. We use polymers to get a soft, low sound or solid steel for a firm, high sound. The hardness and stiffness of the material influences pitch and volume. Head shape also plays a part. Large mallet designs can produce a lot of sound due to the thin sections necessary for spreading out weight to achieve high MOI.

Feel

Although a putter's feel is often tied to the sound it makes at impact, there are other senses that interact with a putter during the stroke that influence the golfer's perception of the putter's feel.

The grip is the only part of the putter that the golfer touches during the stroke. The size and shape of the grip is crucial to ensuring the hands are in a comfortable position. Size and shape can also determine how much the hands contribute to the overall stroke movement. Larger grips rest more in the palms, softening the movement of the hands and putting more emphasis on the shoulders. Smaller grips that sit more in the fingers can free up wrist movement, creating a more complex pendulum stroke. This type of movement is harder to control and is often employed by "feel" players versus "mechanical" players who prefer a simple pendulum stroke.

The putter's balance also influences the golfer's perception of how the putter feels. Over the past 20 years the weight of the average putter head has increased from about 310g to about 355g, for many reasons.

The one we feel is most accurate is the rising preference of golfers to remove the hands from the stroke and rely on a simple pendulum stroke using the shoulders.

As the larger muscles are employed, more head weight is needed in order to better control the head's movement.

As a result of rising head weight, grip weights have increased from about 55g to 75g, to ensure the putter is well-balanced.

Good putter balance is key to executing a smooth stroke, and a smooth and confident stroke is essential to good putting.

Roll

What constitutes a good roll? We define it as when the ball leaves the putter face with very little bouncing, very little skidding, and starts rolling end-over-end as soon as possible. The better a golfer is at achieving this, the better they can control their desired initial ball speed, leading to better distance control. And keen distance control is another key to good putting.

Good roll starts with the direction of the stroke and the putter's dynamic loft at impact.

Our testing shows that golfers who achieve good roll usually have a dynamic loft (the nett loft of the putter at impact, which is the result of combining static loft and shaft lean) of between 1 and 2°.

They also exhibit an upward angle of attack of between 2 and 3°.

This type of motion works with the friction of the ball against the putter face to launch the ball at about a 1 to 2° angle, with topspin.

A 1 or 2° launch angle is necessary to lift the ball out of the small depression in the grass it rests in due to its weight. The topspin helps minimise bouncing, minimise skid distance and start the ball rolling end-over-end sooner.

Friction between the ball and the face helps produce topspin, as long as the loft and motion of the stroke are correct. Getting the launch at the ideal 1 or 2° is important.

A proper putter fitting includes checking launch angle and trying different lofts to achieve this ideal. As putter designers, we enhance friction by developing features that interact with the ball's cover.

These features can be a series of grooves, ovals or other markings with aggressive edges. We can also design inserts that work with the ball to increase the production of topspin. We do this by constructing multi-material inserts, polymers and metals, that will use friction as well as dynamic movement to impart topspin on the ball.

Centre of gravity (CG) position and MOI value also influence spin. A low and deep CG causes a movement in the head during impact that enhances topspin.

By design, mallets have a lower and deeper CG than blade putters. We have seen an increase of as much as 20rpm in topspin in a mallet compared to a blade because of the difference in CG location. That's a significant increase.

Why mallets are increasingly popular

If you have learned anything from this white paper, it's that mallet-style putters have many attributes that promote good and consistent putting. We strive to give our mallets unique and pleasing shapes that inspire confidence.

Mallets often have bold alignment lines and/or features that promote accurate aiming. They usually have high MOI that makes them very forgiving to ensure proper and consistent ball speed on mis-hits.

And a mallet's CG position promotes good roll.

Many of the best players in the world have come to this same conclusion. We have found in our years of designing clubs that game-improvement qualities aren't just for amateurs. Highly skilled players also like the help these features provide.

However, fitting these players correctly is often what gives them the edge they need to perform their best.

A new trend right now is designing features into mallets that have been reserved for blade putters. That includes applying different hosel positions in mallets to change the nature of the head's rotation during the stroke.

In the past, mallets have come in just one hosel style: a shaft with a series of bends to achieve a face-balanced design.

(Note: A face-balanced putter has the shaft axis in line with the putter's centre of gravity as you look at it towards the face.)

This design minimises the amount of head rotation the during a stroke.

This is ideal for beginner golfers who need to minimise and simplify the putter's motion.

However, there are many accomplished golfers who have grown accustomed to a certain amount of rotation. Putting with a design that has a rotational quality that doesn't match your stroke can cause inconsistencies. Installing blade-style hosels into mallet designs allows us to better match head rotation with stroke rotation.

This will benefit those golfers who have, for years, used blade-style putters but desire the performance benefits of a mallet.

At Odyssey, we will continue to strive to make the best putters in the world to help golfers of all skill levels putt at their very best.

We have had our greatest success when we innovate in the six areas described in this white paper.

While we have found mallet-style putters embody these six qualities best of all, we will never lose sight of the fact that many golfers enjoy putting with blade-style putters as well.

We will continue to innovate in hose designs as well. If we keep in mind the Odyssey ethos that has guided us for the past 26 years, we think we will be in a good place.

Chapter 5
GREEN READING

WE all know how to read greens, don't we? Or do we?
In order to hole more putts, shoot lower scores and have more fun on the golf course, we have to be able to read greens or putting surfaces. Agreed?

We have already determined that pace determines line but what do the majority of golfers, from weekend club members to top tour pros focus most of their attention on? Correct – line!

Almost every golfer we see, whether that be in a fun game with friends, a club competition or a major championship, spends the majority of their time trying to figure out the line. If any given putt is, let's say for argument's sake, 90 per cent pace and 10 per cent line, why do we spend 90 per cent of our time focusing on the line?

Countless books and articles have been written and YouTube videos made on reading greens but, again, most of the focus is placed almost entirely on line.

However, if you think about it, as we have mentioned in Chapter 4, the line does not or cannot exist without the correct pace.

So, if pace determines line, what determines pace?

There are numerous contributing factors and considerations which you should be aware of when trying to figure out what the ball needs to do to go in the hole.

Factors such as:

• How long is the putt? Be aware that a breaking putt will travel a

greater distance than a straight putt.
• Have the greens been cut this morning?
• Has the dew been swept from the greens?
• Has it been or is it currently raining?
• Is my putt down grain or into the grain? Anyone who has played golf in South Africa or the Far East will tell you grain can play a massive role in how your golf ball behaves on the green.
• If you are playing late in the afternoon on a warm summer's day, has the grass grown since the green keepers cut the greens in the morning? Yes folks, grass does grow during the day.
• Have the greens retained moisture from overnight rain or the soaking they have had from the pop-up sprinkler system, or has the wind and sunshine dried them out so they become firm and crusty?
• Is the putt uphill or downhill? An uphill putt will generally be slower and break or turn less than its downhill counterpart. This may sound like a fairly obvious statement but we have known top tournament professionals who have struggled to see whether a put is uphill or downhill. Greens can be very subtle. Breaks or borrows on greens aren't always blatantly obvious and clear to see.
• Does it go uphill then downhill? Does it go downhill then flatten out? Is it a straight putt or does it have a left to right break, a left to right break or is it a double-breaker?

These are all considerations when you are figuring out what your ball needs to do to go in the hole.

The clues are there for us all to see but we need to know where to look and how to look for them.

Your brain is like a super computer that is always switched on. We just need to make sure we have it running the correct programme or software at any given time. We have to be aware of how the contours, speed of the green, length of putt, strength of wind and so on will affect how the ball travels to its ultimate destination, the hole.

That's all well and good but how can we actually use what our eyes see and our brain computes to become a great green reader?

Have you ever stood over an iron shot from 150 yards out, or any distance for that matter, looked at the green and thought: "I must try to leave myself an uphill putt because if I'm above the hole, I'm going to have one seriously fast putt."

If you have, you have already started reading the green before you are anywhere near it. You have become aware of where the low side is. Well done.

If you haven't, we suggest you do. We're not saying you should start trying to read subtle breaks or borrows on the green from miles away but please be aware of the green's high and low points. Some greens are relatively flat but most will have high and low points.

As you walk towards the green, you can have your attention on your breath as you do the 'walk' but you can, in the present moment allow information from the green start to work its way into your consciousness. Be gently aware of the topography and look for these high and low points. They are often on diagonal lines - if the highest point of the green is the back left corner, the lowest point may well be the front right corner.

Does the green slope from back to front or front to back? Is it higher on the left side or the right side? Your brain is always switched on, you just need to make sure you are using the correct programme at any given time. Now is the time to put it into green-reading mode.

Once you have determined where the low side is, you can really start to look for the clues that will help you figure out the line but as we already know, more importantly, we can start to look for clues relating to pace.

Think about your current green reading process. Chances are you will mark your ball, give it a clean and when it's your turn to putt, replace it with a line you have drawn on the ball to help align it to your target or intended start line, pointing where you want to go.

We're not massive fans of drawing a line on the ball and we'll explain why in Chapter 6 when we talk about visualisation.

Once you have your ball on the green and your marker in your pocket, you probably crouch down and look down the line of your putt, focusing on the line you want your ball to start and continue on.

Sound familiar? What are you really learning from this and where are you really placing your focused attention? The answers are: not a lot; and the line, despite the fact that pace determines the line.

The importance of reading putts from the low side

We've all the seen or played with the guy who looks at every putt from every angle right? What is he looking for? Basically he's looking for clues that will lead him to make a decision on how hard to hit his putt and what line to hit it on. Line and pace.

We don't recommend that you study every putt from every conceivable angle, a round of golf takes long enough.

However, we do believe you should look at ALL your putts from the LOW side. Whether that is a 30-foot putt or a three-foot putt, always look at it from the low side.

Once you figure out where the low side is, use your eyes and feet to help you here, look at it from around halfway down the length of the putt and three or four paces back from the line.

For example, when faced with a 20-foot putt, walk what you think is 10 feet then take a few steps back.

Be careful not to step on your line or that of your playing partners, especially if you want them to talk to you for the rest of the round!

Crouching down so that your eyes are closer to the ground will help you see the contours a little more clearly but even standing up, you will see a lot more than you will ever see from only looking down the line from behind the ball.

Why is low-side reading so important? The reasons and benefits are numerous.

You will effectively be looking at what you face in 3D HD widescreen. You will see the full picture if you stand far enough back to see both your ball and the hole in your peripheral vision. You will see the full length of the putt. As a general rule, if you have a 10-foot putt, stand halfway down the putt and 10 feet back from your intended approximate line.

If you only look at your putt "down the line", it foreshortens the perceived distance. The chances are your eyes won't actually make contact with the ground until 18 to 24 inches beyond the ball.

This confuses your brain and it starts to compute the required distance, MINUS that 18 to 24 inches. Your brain tells your body how much force to apply, relative to the information it has gathered and your body responds accordingly. When you think about it logically, it makes perfect sense that the resultant putt will probably come up short.

You should also understand and be aware of the fact that a putt with two feet of break will travel further than a straight putt of what would at first glance to be the same length. Not something many golfers tend to factor in when determining the pace of any given putt and how hard to hit it. This makes a big difference and should not be overlooked as it will be a major factor in determining pace.

We introduced this concept to Roger Chapman, a winner on the European Tour and a two-time major winner on the Champions Tour. His response was: "I've played professional golf since 1982 and I can barely get my head round how different putts look from the low side. For a start, a 12-foot putt looks about two feet longer, which would explain why I've been struggling to get the ball up to the hole lately.

"This is a game-changer for me and I can't believe it's taken me until now to incorporate this into my green-reading process – on every putt."

The results were clear to see almost immediately, as Roger then went on a nice run on the European Seniors Tour finishing 16th, 4th, 10th, 5th and 4th in his next five events.

Not only will you start to see the length of the putt in its entirety, you will notice if it is uphill or downhill, something that will have an effect on the speed of your putt and the pace at which you will need to hit it. You will see subtle undulations and changes in elevation, all of which will help with your decision making when it comes to where you hit your putt and how hard you hit it to give your ball the best possible chance of going in the hole.

We cannot stress the importance of this aspect of green-reading strongly enough and we make no apologies if we refer to this throughout the book. It really is that important.

You may well be thinking that that's all well and good but you don't want to take too much time on the greens, and that a round of golf can take too long as it is.

Trust us when we say that this will not add time to your round of golf but actually enable you to play faster.

Really? Yes, really. You can do your detective work while your playing partners are preparing to putt, so that you are truly ready when it is your turn.

Over and above that, because you will now be better equipped to roll your ball on the correct line at the appropriate pace, you will hole more putts, hit your approach putts closer, greatly reduce the number of three putts you have and ultimately spend less time on the greens.

You might have noticed that we don't recommend looking at your putts from the high side. Why? Simply because looking at a putt of any length from the high side creates a bit of an optical illusion and essentially flattens out a lot of the contours that are clearly visible from the low side. Try it for yourself, you'll soon see exactly what we mean. Having said that, taking a look at the last foot of any putt from the high side can help you visualise where your entry point into the hole should be.

"What about looking at the putt from behind the hole looking back towards my ball? I've seen the pros doing that on TV."

This is a question we are often asked and our thoughts are as follows.

Looking at your putt from this angle can help you determine an entry point. However, please understand that your eyes will see the additional distance beyond the hole this will lead to your brain being fooled into thinking you have a greater distance to cover than you have in reality.

It can also look a little different from this angle which can lead to you second-guessing all the information you have gathered from down the line and the low side. Second guessing leads to uncertainty and indecision, which in turn leads to a lack of commitment.

Bernhard Langer, who despite having had his putting issues from time to time, has always been a prolific winner of tournaments once said: "Indecision will, more often than not, have far worse consequences than committing to a wrong decision."

Rarely does a putt lacking in commitment come close to going in the hole never mind finding its way to the bottom of the cup.

Take a moment to reflect on your recent putting rounds. Chances are that when you replay the last three or four rounds you have played in your mind, you'll probably think 'if only I hadn't missed those putts' or 'I left so many shots out there today because of my putting'.

If you are extremely diligent, you might just head over to the putting green to work on your putting but please don't fall into the same old trap of only working on your stroke with your start-line training aids and gadgets.

All too often we blame our technique or stroke for our putting shortfalls, when in actual fact, you have most probably struggled with line and pace because you haven't read the greens properly.

The importance of creating putts

When was the last time you walked off the course thinking that was about the very best you could have scored today, thanks to your superior putting skills?

Our aim is to help you do just that by understanding and, more importantly, applying the concepts and principles outlined in this book.

If you don't apply them, you may well have enjoyed the read but you must apply what you have learned and are continuing to learn in order to make a real and measurable difference. If you always do what you've always done, you'll always get what you've always got.

In essence, we suggest you spend less time working on the mechanics of your stroke, trying out a new way to hold the putter with a thicker or thinner grip, stressing about the start line, changing putters as often as you change your socks and spend a bit more time actually practising how to read greens.

We know this will make a massive and measurable difference. The number of putts you take during any given round of golf and ultimately your scores and therefore your enjoyment will testify to that.

There are green reading systems and methods that have been taught over the years and the guys at Aim-Point have created a strong following and very successful business around their concepts and methodology. You have probably seen tour pros on TV closing one eye and holding up a finger or two to figure out the line, which is all part of their green reading process. As with any method or system, if it works for you, keep doing it. We're not suggesting you stop using it, far from it.

We are, however, suggesting that if you incorporate the principles outlined in this book, you will greatly enhance your chances of becoming a better creator of putts.

We prefer the concept of "creating putts" rather than tying yourself in technical knots and mental clutter in a bid to perfect your stroke. What does a perfect putting stroke look like anyway? As far as we are concerned, it's one that gets the ball to disappear into the hole on the right line at the right pace.

We've all seen golfers with technically sound putting strokes. Some are good putters and others look like they should be but aren't. Why is that? The ones who look like they should hole lots of putts but don't are either not great at reading greens, struggle with line and pace, or have their attention somewhere other than on what the ball needs to do to go in the hole.

The ones who do hole a lot of putts successfully combine their technical skills with all the other aspects we talk about throughout this book. They let the putt create the stroke, not the other way round.

Historically, great putters become great putters because they believe they are going to hole their fair share of putts.

When Tiger Woods was at his peak, which was close to an astonishing 20-year period, he appeared to have the ability to will his ball into the hole from all sorts of distances and directions. More than that, he did it when he needed to, time and time again. Do you think he was any good at reading greens and that he allowed the putt to determine the stroke?

Tiger was a fantastic putter. He knew it, and his opponents and fellow competitors knew it. When it came to the back nine of a tournament, everyone expected Tiger to hole putts and make a charge up the leaderboard.

Tiger expected to hole putts and so did everyone else. It was great for his psyche and undoubtedly unsettled his fellow competitors.

What made him so good? Yes, he was technically proficient but, ultimately, he could read greens like a wizard, his pace was as good as anyone who has ever played the game and ultimately he knew what the ball had to do to go in the hole.

Tiger probably holed more crucial putts at crucial moments than anyone else in the modern game. He was arguably the greatest creator of putts we have ever seen.

He completely understood the importance of green reading, worked extremely hard and smartly to learn all he could about how the contours and conditions would affect his ball and ultimately, excelled at it.

Between 2002 and 2005, Tiger faced 1,540 putts of three feet and in on the PGA Tour. He missed only three of them! That is not a misprint, he missed only three of them!

"I believe my creative mind is my greatest weapon." – Tiger Woods, winner of 14 major championships, 18 WGC tournaments and 79 PGA Tour events.

Three exercises

The art of green reading is not a skill you can learn immediately or from the pages of a book, not even this one! However, by applying the principles outlined here, you can and will become a whole lot better at it over time.

They say there is no substitute for experience and in this instance, we couldn't agree more.

Every golf club on the planet has a member who claims to know every blade of grass on every green like the back of his hand. While this may not be quite true literally, there is every chance he knows the greens better than most because he has putted on them more frequently than most.

More importantly, he has spent time learning the subtle breaks and borrows, the slight changes in elevation and he definitely knows where the low side is on each and every green.

Unfortunately, most practice putting greens tend to be relatively flat. Not all but most. We've never quite figured out why this should be. Surely the practice putting green should replicate the greens on the golf course? They are after all, or certainly should be, designed to help you prepare for what you are about to encounter on the golf course.

If the putting green at your home course is relatively flat and the greens are not, you probably won't be able to learn a whole lot about green reading, regardless of how much time you spend on it. That doesn't mean you should give up on your quest to become a great reader of greens. Far from it.

Every day is a school day and you never stop learning, so whenever you are out on the golf course, whether that be in a relaxed game with friends or family, a club competition or a major championship, use that time wisely. Learn what you can from every putt you hit. Remember how your ball reacted. Store that information for the future.

Top tournament professionals (who tend to be pretty good putters) and caddies take great care and time during practice rounds to study the greens, figure out where the pin positions might be for the rest of the tournament and take notes. Lots of notes. They also have the benefit of incredibly detailed yardage books and many are now using The Green Book which charts the length and direction of every slope and change in elevation. You name it, they'll incorporate it into their extremely detailed maps of the greens.

Exercise 1: Looking For Clues

We mentioned earlier on in this section that your brain is like a super computer that is always switched on and all we have to do is to ensure we are running the correct programme at the relevant time.

Look for clues. Look for high points and low points, especially the low side.

We introduced this concept to one of our younger students and explained that the clues were everywhere, you just need to know where to look.

"The clues are on the ground," we said. His response? "Actually, the clues ARE the ground." Pretty good answer for a 12-year-old, don't you think?

Exercise 2: Can You Feel It?

Don't underestimate your senses. As you walk around the green, be aware of any changes in elevation through your feet. You may well do this already. If you do, you are one step ahead, pardon the pun. If you don't, next time you go out to play, pay attention to the feedback provided by your feet as you approach your ball as you walk on to the green. Are you walking uphill or downhill? Is your weight going to the outside of your right foot or your left foot? The more you do this, the more it becomes second nature. Information is power: application of that information is where the real power lies.

Exercise 3: Play To Learn

We are great believers in playing to learn rather than learning to play. Ask any great player where they learned to play and 99 per cent will reply 'on the golf course'.

We are not saying you should avoid the practice putting green and do all your practice on the golf course. Nor are we saying that you take everything you have learned from this book and spend forever on every putt on every green each time you play golf. Be aware of others on the golf course and try not to hold up play. Especially if the four guys waiting in the fairway in the group behind are bigger than you! Practise your processes on the putting green, then apply them on the course.

When playing to learn, choose your moments. Find out when the course is going to be quiet. The last two hours of daylight are the perfect time to do some detective work on the greens. The course is more likely to be relatively quiet and the setting sun casts fantastic shadows, highlighting all the subtle undulations of the putting surfaces.

It may also be very beneficial from a brain perspective to do some practice at night close to the time you go to sleep.

There is new scientific evidence to support that learning is consolidated during sleep.

Researchers who analysed brain activity in sleeping volunteers who had learned to navigate through a computer-generated virtual town have discovered evidence that spatial memories are consolidated during deep sleep.

Developing feel for pace is essentially improving your spatial awareness.

The correlation between what I do here with the putter and what happens out there with the ball.

Also, the researchers say that they have shown for the first time that the activity level in the brain's learning centre, the hippocampus, correlates with the improvement in memory performance when the subjects are tested the next day.

According to Philippe Peigneux and his colleagues: "A growing body of experimental evidence shows the influence of sleep on the consolidation of recent memory traces. The underlying hypothesis posits that the information that is acquired during wakefulness is actively altered, restructured, and strengthened during sleep."

So, practising your putting late at night is not only a wonderful calming experience it is potentially a great time to consolidate learning and memory.

We cannot stress the importance playing to learn strongly enough. Great putters become great putters by playing golf and holing putts for birdies, pars and bogeys when it matters.

Yes, we want you to work on and apply all the principles we talk about on these pages on the putting green. That is where you can practice your process and that is where you take what you have learned from your play on the course but ultimately we play golf on a golf course, not on a practice range or putting green.

Key takeaways

1 As you walk towards the green, be aware of the topography and look for these high and low points. They are often on diagonal lines – if the highest point of the green is the back left corner, the lowest point may well be the front right corner.

2 Low-side green-reading offers numerous reasons and benefits. You will effectively be looking at what you face in 3D HD widescreen. You will see the full picture if you stand far enough back to see both your ball and the hole in your peripheral vision.

3 All too often we blame our technique or stroke for our putting shortfalls, when in actual fact, we have most probably struggled with line and pace because we haven't read the greens properly.

4 Spend less time working on the mechanics of your stroke, trying out a new way to hold the putter with a thicker or thinner grip, stressing about the start line and changing putters as often as you change your socks. Instead, spend a bit more time actually practising how to read greens.

5 Ask two questions, look for clues on line and pace from the low side and start holing putts.

6 Get out onto the course late at night. It is a wonderful time to let the shadows on the green assist your detective work. Also the nearer you learn something to sleep time the better the learning is consolidated.

7 We want you to be able to personalise what you learn from this book and take ownership of it. Only then can you truly progress and become the great putter we know you can be. Our ultimate aim is to empower you to unleash your true putting potential, hole more putts, shoot lower scores and have more fun on the course.

THE SURFACES
WE PUTT ON

W ITH all this talk of putting, technology and custom-fitted putters, we thought it might be an idea to talk about the surfaces we are going to putt on.

While we may have been fortunate enough to have visited and played on hundreds of golf courses around the world, we do not claim to be experts on greens or putting surfaces.

Thankfully we know a man who is.

Steve Cram, golf courses manager at Archerfield Links, which is situated at the very heart of Scotland's Golf Coast in East Lothian just a short drive from Scotland's capital city of Edinburgh, has won numerous awards and many admirers throughout his 30-plus years as a greenkeeper.

We may all have opinions on why the greens at our local course aren't always as we might like them to be but we are great believers in leaving course maintenance, set-up and preparation to the experts. Those who actually have the relevant experience and qualifications.

We all want to play on true rolling fast greens "just like the tour pros do". Or at least that's what we think we want. Having been to Augusta National for the Masters, we can assure you that, while the idea of putting on Augusta's greens is enormously attractive, the reality is somewhat different.

Not because they aren't amazing – they are.

However, their undulations and speed make them almost unplayable for mere mortals. Figuring out line and pace become much, much more difficult than hitting fairways and greens. They really are the ultimate challenge and when the best players in the world hole putts on them, they really do deserve all the applause they receive.

Without dwelling on Augusta for too long, the reasons their

greens are immaculate every April in readiness for the Masters are numerous. They have a massive team of experts, they have more funds and machinery than most small countries and they have pretty good growing conditions due to their geographical location.

Greenkeeping teams are the unsung heroes of the golf industry and, in our opinion, they rarely receive the credit or help they deserve.

We can all help our greenkeeping team by doing our bit fixing pitch marks.

Fix your own and one more and every green you ever play on will benefit directly as a result. We all know that unprepared pitch marks are unsightly and create uneven surfaces.

As Steve puts it: "Not repairing pitchmarks or repairing them incorrectly is akin to leaving an open wound which is therefore susceptible to disease."

Never thought of it that way? Neither had we!

Next time you play, take a moment to appreciate the hard work your greenkeeping team do and help them by repairing couple of pitch marks on each and every green. It's the best way to create smooth putting surfaces and prevent that "open wound" from becoming infected.

Steve is a fantastic course manager and he and his team are doing a great job at Archerfield, which has gained an envious international reputation as a golf destination of tremendous note despite only having opened for play in 2004.

Steve is a low-handicap golfer himself and the work he carries out on both the Fidra and Dirleton Links at Archerfield is done very much through the eyes of a golfer first and foremost.

His desire to "get things just right" is infectious. Good is never good enough and he works tirelessly to present every aspect of the courses as well as he can. Whether that be the practice facilities, tees, fairways, bunkers or greens complexes.

The art (and challenges) of greenkeeping
With Steve Cram, course manager at Archerfield Links

"Looking after the courses here is a pleasure and a privilege. I love golf and love to play the game as much as anyone. My ultimate aim is to prepare the golf courses to the best of my ability to allow golfers of all standards to enjoy their game whether that be in a relaxed game with friends, the club championship or a European Tour event.

My profession is greenkeeping but my passion is playing golf and I want to be able to play either course when it looks and plays it very best.

"As course manager, you have to have a master plan both long and short term and, just like golf, it is essential to adapt to what is in front of you at any given moment.

"Sometimes plans can't be executed quite as planned due to ever-changing weather conditions which can be challenging.

"Unfortunately, there are some golfers who don't understand that grass needs to be constantly cared for and the kind of grasses that grow in certain parts of the world can only survive in certain conditions which is always a consideration when planting and seeding.

"We have to be realistic about what can be achieved and what grasses can grow in a manner sustainable for the environment wherever you are in the world. Certain climates better lend themselves to growing certain types of grasses. We have to be aware of that and do all we can to ensure that we combine grasses that get along.

"For example, poa annua (annual meadow grass) and bent tend to blend quite well.

"Grass needs, water, warmth and sunlight to thrive and if the soil temperature drops below 10°C, sustainable growth is unachievable.

"Each individual green requires individual attention depending on the environment it sits in.

"Is it surrounded by trees? Does it sit in a low-lying area of the course? Is it more or less exposed to wind and sunshine than others?

"All these are major considerations if we are to present the golfer with consistent putting surfaces.

"In order to create fast greens, there are certain things we can do to encourage that including the height of cut, aeration which degrades the thatch regeneration process and top dressing which keeps thatch open and acts like a filter to allow water to drain properly.

"The relatively recent introduction of turf irons allow greenkeepers to essentially iron greens to increase speed without dropping the cut height too low.

"Moisture is probably the biggest influencer on pace. Think about how quickly greens can slow up after a heavy shower."

Chapter 6
VISUALISATION

"**I** NEVER hit a bad shot or a bad putt in my mind before I hit it," says Jack Nicklaus, arguably the greatest golfer of all time, winner of 18 major championships, 79 PGA Tour events and a grand total of 117 professional victories.

Essentially, what Jack is saying here is that before he hit any shot or putt, he had an extremely clear picture of what his ball needed to do to create the desired outcome before he hit it.

He doesn't talk about golf swings or putting strokes, he talks about shots and putts. Can you see where we're going here?

What he saw when visualising his putts as part of his pre-shot routine was, yes, you guessed it, the ball rolling into the hole on the right line at exactly the right pace.

So why is visualisation so powerful and important?

Basically, if you can't see a good putt in your imagination, you'll probably find it very difficult to create a putt that travels on the right line at the appropriate pace and disappears into the hole. With a clear image of what you want the ball to actually do helps create a 'map of movement' for your body to follow.

As with every other section in this book, it all relates back to attention and our Two Questions in Chapter 3: Is it possible for the ball to go in the hole, and what does the ball need to do to go in the hole?

By asking these two questions, you can create a crystal-clear intention, which in turn allows you to direct your focused attention to the task in hand, creating a putt that finishes in the bottom of the cup.

Do you currently visualise what you are about to do before you hit your putts?

Whether your answer is yes or no, this section will be a game changer for you. It was for us and for hundreds of golfers who have attended our Putting Performance Principles Schools and Master-classes.

"In practice rounds, I always checked the slopes and grain," said Gordon Brand Jnr. "So I knew where to put the ball on the green with my approach shots. As a result, I was very aware of what kind of putts I was likely to have, so my visualisation started long before getting to the green.

"Once on the green, I was always pretty quick, looking at where I wanted the ball to fall into the hole at the right pace.

"My first look and instincts were right 99 per cent of the time. It was important to then just let it go. Less was always more," he said.

If you do use visualisation as part of your pre-shot routine when putting, what do you see?
• Do you see the ball rolling towards and into the hole?
• Do you see a start line or an entry point?
• Do you see how the slopes and changes in elevation of the green will help your ball reach its intended target?
• Do you commit to what you see initially or do you second-guess yourself?
• Do you see a continuous line or a dotted line?
• If you see a line, what colour is it?
• Is it a thick line or a thin line? How thick or thin is it?
Be prepared to play around with the images.

Become the 'attention detective' in the sense that you become very aware of what you as a unique individual need to pay attention to so you can release your true abilities.

Why we are wary of drawing a line on your ball

In Chapter 5, where we looked at green reading, we mentioned that we weren't big fans of drawing a line on the ball to use as a start-line aid. Here are the reasons why.

Have you ever taken great care when replacing your ball on the green after marking it to ensure the line you have drawn on your ball matches up with your intended start line? Probably.

Have you ever then gone to address your ball and thought 'wait a minute, that doesn't look to be pointing where I thought it was'? Probably.

Have you then started to second guess your initial read? Probably.

Have you then not committed fully to that putt as a result because you are caught in two minds? Again, probably.

Have you then left that putt short as a direct result? Almost definitely. We're not saying this definitely will happen if you draw a line on your ball as a start-line aid but we are saying it can and sometimes does happen. This can be as a result of your eye position which can alter according to how your neck bends or rotates, potentially creating a disconnect between what you saw when you were lining your ball up and what you see when you address it.

If you do draw a line on your ball and you see a line of the path the ball will travel to the hole in your mind's eye, chances are that the line you see will be an extension of the line on your ball.

That line you see will be a very, very thin one. This tells your brain you have to roll your ball along that thin line.

Think of it like walking along a tightrope. How comfortable, confident or relaxed would you be about that? Unless you are a highly skilled and vastly experienced tightrope walker, 'comfortable', 'confident' and 'relaxed' are probably the last words you would use to describe how you would feel in that situation.

For years, golfers have used a builder's chalk line as a training aid and focused their attention on rolling their ball along that incredibly thin line. If the ball falls off that line, even if it ends up in the hole, that would be regarded as a failure as the task was to keep the ball on the chalk line. Some might say that golf is a game of precision and practising to be extremely precise is definitely the way forward.

If it works for you then carry on. However, if it doesn't we suggest you use two chalk lines.

One on the left edge of the hole and one 4.25 inches directly opposite on the right edge of the hole. You can also put your alignment rods to good use here to create the same visual aid.

Suddenly your line has gone from being as thin as a razor's edge to as wide as the hole itself. What would be easier, putting along the tightrope, or putting down a 4.25-inch-wide channel?

We introduced this concept to one of the very good amateur golfers we work with and asked him to tell us what he saw. His answer was one we loved so much, we have since incorporated it into our coaching.

"I see a length of guttering that starts at my ball and finishes right in the middle of the hole. If I can roll my ball down that gutter, I can't miss." Barry Hobson, we thank you for that.

Focusing on the thin line puts your attention almost entirely on line, whereas giving yourself the entire width of the hole, frees up your mind and your muscles and allows you to focus on... you guessed it, pace.

Is the line really as wide as the hole? Absolutely! If you get the pace right.

The clever people at Hawk-Eye Innovations, probably better known for their work in tennis to determine whether the ball is in or out, have created a system that allows golf broadcasters to project an image on the screen of the line the ball needs to travel on to go in the hole.

If you look closely, you will see that line varies in thickness, depending on the pace the golfer hits his putt. If you look really closely, you will notice that the line is always at least as wide as the hole itself.

Have you ever visualised the line being as wide as the hole? Neither had 99 per cent of our students but once they started to see that much wider, thicker line, they were amazed at how easy it is to hole putts and you will be too.

While we're on the subject of width or thickness of line, if that line had a colour, what colour would it be? Initially, most people struggle to see a line that is at least as wide as the hole. Why? Quite simply because they have never looked for it before. Our good friends at PuttView have created an amazing augmented reality system for practice and training that uses this very concept which is genius in it's simplicity.

Think of your favourite colour or a colour that would stand out against the green of the putting surface. It could be black, it could be white, it could be yellow, it could in fact be any colour you choose. Try closing your eyes and experimenting with different colours in your imagination. You will soon find one that stands out vividly against the green.

Prior to winning his second WGC event at Firestone Country Club in Akron Ohio, Darren Clarke was struggling to find inspiration on the greens. Late one night at his own club at the time Queenwood in London we had a discussion about 'seeing the line' and he admitted to finding it a struggle.

'Darren, if the line into the hole had a colour, what would it be?', I asked. With the look that only Darren could give, he gave it some thought and looked at a putt.

'Red, I suppose' came the less than enthusiastic answer.

'Ok let's see what that does'.

The first putt, a 20-footer, rolled purely towards the hole and just died into the hole on the top side. A couple more putts drained into the cup. Darren smiled and said: 'We may be on to something here!' A couple of weeks later rounds of 65, 70, 66 and 67 blew away a high-quality field of the world's best players, including the then-dominant Tiger Woods.

If you think about it logically, your golf ball, at 1.68 inches in diameter doesn't even take up half the width of that newly introduced 4.25 inch line.

That being the case, there is actually room for at least two golf balls to fit into the hole.

In fact, there is actually enough room for three golf balls, if they are hit on different lines at different paces. One falling in the high side with a lot of break and just enough pace. One going in just right of centre on a right-to-left breaking putt or just left of centre on a left-to-right breaking putt, on a slightly straighter line with a little more pace.

There is also the stunt-man route going right in the centre on an even straighter line with even more pace.

We call this the stunt-man route because you have to be extremely brave with little regard for the consequences to take this line. That said, some great putters over the years have enjoyed enormous success putting this way.

As the line changes according to the pace you hit your putt, so does your entry point.

For example, if you take the high line with less pace and a lot of break, your entry point is going to be on the right side of the hole on a right-to-left putt. The more break or borrow you allow for the more your entry point moves from the centre of the hole. This is something you will have to consider when visualising what the ball has to do in order to allow gravity to do its thing and pull your ball into the hole.

Make sure your visualised putts end up in the hole

Always ensure the line and pace you visualise actually makes it as far as the hole. This may sound like we're stating the obvious but experience tells us that even some of the best players in the world don't actually visualise the ball or line disappearing into the hole.

When we ask our students to draw a line to the hole on a piece of paper, rarely does that line get beyond or even as far as the front edge of the hole.

One great visual we love is to imagine the line as a liquid one, pouring into the hole with enough pace to make it to the middle of the hole and not just drip over the front edge or entry point. Imagine liquid mercury being poured along the green and disappearing into the middle of the hole. We do implore you not to actually try this, we don't want you being chased out of town by the greenkeeping staff!

Another very clear visual is to imagine taking a 4.25-inch wide paint brush, dipping it in a tin of paint, the choice of colour is entirely up to you, then painting a line along the green on which you want your ball to travel. Imagining that thicker line which is at least as wide as the hole, reduces tension and frees up your body and mind to enable your instincts and motor skills take over. That is the point when you start to hole more putts than you ever imagined. That is when the fun really begins!

We will end with quotes from two greats of philosophy – Buddha and Phil Price.

"What you think, you become. What you imagine, you create." – Buddha.

"Once I have a clear image of what the ball needs to do to go in the hole, I make sure I am comfortable at address and in my mind. I then like to look at the hole and react to the information I have gathered on line and pace with no mechanical thoughts." – Phil Price, three-time winner on the European Tour, winner on the European Seniors Tour and the man who holed that amazing putt on the 16th green at The Belfry to defeat Phil Mickelson 3&2 in the 2002 Ryder Cup.

Getting ready to putt

Visualisation is an extremely powerful and useful skill that is used in many sports but rarely talked about in golf. In fact, we can't think of a sport or pursuit where visualisation wouldn't be useful.

With 91 Grand Prix victories and seven World Championship titles, Michael Schumacher was one of the greatest Formula One racing drivers in the history of the sport.

Schumacher was known to sit in his car before every race with his eyes closed. He used that pre-race time to quieten his mind and visualise every inch of the racing line he wanted to take.

For him, this was a form of meditation that allowed him to get into The Zone. A place where he could operate on an intuitive level. He may well have been asking his own two questions: Is it possible to win the race? And what does my car need to do to cross the finishing line ahead of everyone else. Line and pace perhaps?

Enough fantasising about chequered flags and spraying champagne over an adoring crowd, let's get back to putting and visualisation.

Once again, in order to make a difference, you have to ask the Two Questions. Once you have determined that, yes, it is possible for the ball to go in the hole and that the ball needs to travel on the correct line at the appropriate pace, you can start green reading.

When you are comfortable and confident that you have gathered the relevant information required to perform the task in hand – holing the putt you face – now you can turn your attention to visualisation.

Thin line or thick line?

Are you putting along a tightrope or down a gutter? As we mentioned earlier, if you draw a line on your ball, regardless of how thin or thick it is, you are likely to see a continuation of that line in your mind's eye.

By all means use a line to help you align the middle of the ball with the sweet spot on your putter but remember the line your ball will travel on is always at least as thick or as wide as the hole if you get the pace right. One of our favourite drills to reinforce this is to use alignment rods to practise creating a strong visual of just how wide the line is.

Place a rod or a golf club or shaft on either side of the hole.

Start with some straight three-foot putts and experience the freedom that the new, much thicker line creates in both your mind and your muscles. Remember, tension is not your friend and a busy mind creates tension. This wider line quietens your mind, allowing you to place your focused attention on pace and letting you make a free-flowing, instinctive stroke.

If you are putting down the tightrope we referred to, you will probably experience an increase in tension in your grip – not helpful.

You will also invite an increase in the number of thoughts running through your mind – even less helpful.

Remember what we said about a single point of focused attention? When you have three or four thoughts in your mind, all vying for your attention, unconsciously you will try to act on each and every one of them. As a putting stroke typically lasts between 1.5 and 1.8 seconds, it is virtually impossible to think clearly about any more than one thing during that very short time.

Choose a colour

Close your eyes and try to see a nice thick line. Depending on what kind of putt you are trying to create in your mind's eye, that line can be straight or curved. The choice is yours. Do you see that line in a specific colour? Whether it is black, white, yellow, blue or red is largely irrelevant. It's all about what YOU see, not what we recommend you see.

Now open your eyes and apply that colour to the thick line you see when you are standing over a putt. Try it with long and short putts. What do you experience when you have the freedom to putt your ball along that thick line? We're pretty confident you'll find it liberating, safe in the knowledge you no longer have to worry about putting down that tightrope. Knowing you have a little margin for error will free up your body and mind and allow you to stroke the ball freely into the hole.

The paintbrush

When working with one of our students on some visualisation drills, we asked him to describe what he saw. Without hesitation, he replied: "I see a thick and vivid line on the green as if it had been applied by a paintbrush that was as wide as the hole for the entire length of the putt." Whether that paintbrush line starts at the ball and continues to the middle of the hole or works from the middle of the hole and works back to your ball isn't important.

Experiment with this and other visual aids and if you have any that work for you, we would ask you to do two things: If it works, keep doing it; and let us know!

We promise to give you the appropriate credit when sharing your thoughts in the future.

Trust your instincts – see and do

Pick up a golf ball and either roll or throw it to a specific point or hole on the putting green. Before you do it, think of what the ball needs to do to reach your intended target. Do you see the ball rolling to its destination in your mind's eye before you perform this simple task? Hopefully you will. Did you think about what your hand/arm/shoulder or any other parts had to do? Hopefully and probably not. Did you perform the task pretty well? Hopefully and probably yes. Did you trust your instincts. Absolutely!

Your instincts have probably served you pretty well in your daily life thus far, so why not allow them and your subconscious mind to perform this relatively straightforward task?

"Once I am comfortable with my set up and alignment, I like to look at the hole while I have a practice stroke and react to what I see with no mechanical or technical thoughts," said Phil Price.

Rory McIlroy won the Arnold Palmer Invitational at Bay Hill in March 2018, after making birdies on five of his last six holes for a three-shot victory. Having gone through what for Rory was a prolonged barren spell of eighteen months without a win, he talked about a "perfect round of golf". Perhaps more importantly, he attributed his change in fortunes to improved putting. Having used his putter only 24 times in a final round of 64, he said: "I just wanted to free things up mentally and become more instinctive. I focused a lot less on mechanics. I used a lot of visualisation and reacting to targets.

"I'm trying to get back to feeling how I did as a kid, where your instinct takes over."

Wise words. For the record, his Strokes Gained statistics (for more on strokes gained, we recommend reading Every Shot Counts by Mark Broadie) were as follows:

Off the tee: 31st (1.411)

Approaches to greens: 13th (4.569)

Around the greens: 20th (1.966)

Putting: 1st (10.027)

McIlroy isn't alone in his thinking. Justin Rose echoed Rory's thoughts after finishing fifth at the Valspar Championship the week before a 5th place finish at Bay Hill.

Rose said: "I don't nit-pick every single stroke I make anymore." On viewing putting as less of a science, he said: "I focus more on what I call skill acquisition, which is read, speed and other skills.

"You can have the perfect stroke but you're not necessarily going to make putts."

This train of thought has enabled Rose to focus on "the art form of putting and not obsess too much about the technique."

This change of heart and direction also enabled Rose to win the Fort Worth Invitational at Colonial. He duly climbed into the top five in strokes gained in putting midway through the 2018 PGA Tour season, having ranked outside the top 100 in the same category every year since 2012.

Key takeaways

1 If you do draw a line on your ball and you see a line of the path the ball will travel to the hole in your mind's eye, chances are that the line you see will be an extension of the line on your ball. That line you see will be a very, very thin one. This tells your brain you have to roll your ball along that thin line.
Think of it like walking along a tightrope. How comfortable, confident or relaxed would you be about that? Unless you are a highly skilled and vastly experienced tightrope walker, comfortable, confident and relaxed are probably the last words you would use to describe how you would feel in that situation.

2 Focusing on a thin line puts your attention almost entirely on line, whereas giving yourself the entire width of the hole frees up your mind and your muscles and allows you to focus on the pace. The line is as wide as the hole if you get the pace right.

3 A golf ball, at 1.68 inches in diameter, doesn't even take up half the width of that newly introduced 4.25-inch line. There is actually enough room for three golf balls, if they are hit on different lines at different paces: One falling in the high side with a lot of break and just enough pace; one going in just right of centre on a right-to-left breaking putt or just left of centre on a left-to-right breaking putt; and right in the centre on an even straighter line with even more pace.

4 Always ensure the line and pace you visualise actually makes it as far as the hole. To see the ball 'pouring into the hole' is a good phrase to help with the imagery.

5 Your instincts have probably served you pretty well in your daily life thus far, so why not allow them and your subconscious mind to perform this relatively straightforward task?

VISUALISING
THE LINE OF A PUTT
With PuttView technologies

THROUGHOUT this book we refer to visualisation as one of the key putting performance principles of the lost art of putting. While we know that many great players down the years have used this particular skill to enhance their performance on the putting surfaces, we also understand that not everyone who plays this great game can create a clear picture in their mind's eye of what the ball needs to do to go in the hole.

Jordan Spieth, an exceptional putter, rarely talks about his putting stroke but often talks about "seeing the movie of the putt".

The late, great Seve Ballesteros had perhaps the most vivid imagination in the history of the game on and around the greens.

He saw and played shots others could never imagine let alone execute. He was regarded as having incredible "feel" with a putter in his hands – but in order to feel or create any given putt, he had to visualise it first.

Standing on the 18th green of the Old Course at St Andrews with a 15-foot putt to win the 1984 Open Championship, having figured out the line and pace, he set his ball in motion. As it curved left, it dropped into the hole at the perfect pace, just as he had visualised it. His reaction is one that will be remembered for decades but without that perfect putt, which he first visualised and then created, his famous celebration would never have happened.

Do you sometimes struggle to visualise line and pace? Can you see the line clearly but perhaps your vision of the pace is a little less vivid? Wouldn't it be great if you could see the projected line and pace of a putt when you were practising?

We certainly do, and that's why we went to visit our friends Christoph Preziger and Lukas Posniak at PuttView in Hamburg, Germany, to see, discuss and experience their amazing and ground-breaking technology. We say ground-breaking because, to our knowledge, there is nothing that comes close to being able to project real-time images on to a putting green with what they call their "visual toolbox for practice and training".

Most putting training aids and technology tend to focus on the player and putter, but this is so radically different that we felt compelled to share their concepts with you.

The PuttView team and concept

Christoph has been an ambitious golfer for 15 years. During putting practice, he has often thought about how much it would help him if he could see the ideal path of a putt.

Being an engineer, he knew this path could be calculated for any terrain. In fact, the path has frequently been shown on television.

However this was not of any help to the individual player.

With Christoph, we discussed how we could make this path visually available for the player. One of the major requirements was that the path should be visualised on the green during practice to enable the player to use it as a reference and for feedback.

The PuttView story
By Lukas Posniak and Christoph Preziger of PuttView Technology

During our research we came across Augmented Reality technologies, which were still in the early stages in 2015.

We started working on the first concepts in close collaboration with Professor Frank Steinicke, an expert in the field of Augmented Reality and Human-Computer Interaction. Backed up by government funding, we started our journey at the University of Hamburg. Augmented Reality is a technology of the future and enables you to display any information in your surroundings.

That is exactly what we needed for PuttView, but we also saw potential in the technology beyond golf and even beyond sports.

That is why we named our company Viewlicity, a combination of 'view' and 'simplicity'.

The long-term vision that drives us is to make it easier to learn difficult tasks or processes – such as putting.

There is a lot more technology to PuttView than just Augmented Reality. Actually the system requires four major components to work: An accurate 3D-Model of the green, an algorithm to calculate the ideal putting path, a display device and a way for coaches and players to interact with the system.

The first step to install a PuttView system on a green is to capture a 3D-model of it. We mostly rely on laser scanners for that. Without any dramatic changes in the green you only need to do that once before installing the system, as indoor greens change very little over time. As an alternative to static indoor greens, PuttView also works with all major computer-controlled moving greens that are available. In that case, we calculate an accurate 3D-Model from the position of the jacks and adapt the model inside the software in real-time to the current contour of the green. To account for the speed of the green, we simply stimp the turf and use that value as a parameter in our software.

Once the 3D-Model is saved in our software, PuttView is able to calculate any putt on that surface.

The user can change the starting position, hole location and the speed of the putt to his liking. It was of particular importance to us to design the software and algorithms in a way that the user remains flexible to use it, e.g. setting the distance past hole for his putts.

To display the ideal path on the green we use a projector that is mounted to the ceiling. Depending on the size of the green we would like to cover, we use one or two projectors. People often ask us what the requirements are and how difficult it is to install and our answer usually is it is comparable to a golf simulator.

The major difference is that we need to accurately calibrate the projector to the green surface to ensure the lines match the slopes perfectly.

Last but not least, the user needs an interface to interact with the PuttView system. We developed a tablet application for that purpose which communicates with the PuttView system and enables the user to control all available features and settings. But we consider the tablet application to be more than just a remote control for the system. We believe our system is redefining the way coaches and players interact by opening up a way of visual communication and think this will change the way putting is taught.

While projection-based Augmented Reality is a perfect fit for indoor environments, the future of Augmented Reality lies in AR-headsets. We have already built a first version of PuttView Outdoor using Microsoft's Hololens.

The technology was first demonstrated at the Porsche European Open 2017 and was well received by coaches, tour pros and visitors alike. It may still be a couple of years until this technology becomes more affordable, but it has the potential to become a technology which is being used as frequent as smartphones are today.

A very frequent question we hear when talking to people about PuttView is what kind of speed we recommend to hit a putt at. The answer is quite simple: none in particular. PuttView offers the opportunity to display various speeds for one given putt by setting the distance past hole. Each player is different and tends to hit putts at a different speed. At the same time courses and greens are different and it is important for players to adapt to it, also in terms of what speed you hit a put at.

PuttView enables players to practice putts according to their preference or practice the same putt with different distances past the hole to improve their variability in speed.

Everyone knows that you learn best when addressing as many senses as possible. A lot of players actually imagine a putt in their mind's eye before playing it or imagine a certain target while playing it: However, while developing PuttView we quickly found out that there are different preferences on how the information should be displayed.

For example, you can display the path of the ball, animate it in ball speed, show only parts of the line or the hole entry point. Similarly you can show the aimline, the aimpoint or variations of it. All those options are available in PuttView today and you can use them to find out what image in your mind's eye suits you best for picturing a putt and where your attention should be at while putting. Simply go through the different visuals, play a few putts and see where you perform best. Use the images that worked best for you to improve your routine and focus your attention on while putting.

But we did not want to limit PuttView to the features we have thought of and implemented. We have always thought of it as a visual toolbox for putting practice and wanted it to be flexible in terms of how it can be used. Therefore we included not only various options to change the visuals, but also to create your own. You can think of it as "Paint", which you probably know from your windows computer, for your putting green. Using this sketch function you can draw on the greens, create shapes and patterns on it and save the sketches for later use in another session.

This provides coaches an efficient tool to use the visuals they consider best. At the same time it reduces their preparation time as they do not need to rely on typical aids such as a string or chalk and can reuse the sketches for multiple sessions.

Everyone knows that putting practice is not always the most fun thing to practice. Feedback from our users, and kids in particular, shows us that PuttView adds an engaging component to putting practice. Using the predefined drills or games is a lot more fun than just playing random putts and not receiving any feedback. We will continue adding more content to PuttView and hope to encourage people to spend more time on the putting green."
Christoph Preziger, PuttView

What PuttView does

One of the things Christoph was missing during practice was a way to analyse his mistakes and improve his putting. It was often difficult to figure out what he got wrong: the read, the starting direction or the speed. PuttView displays the path, aimline and pace of any putt on any green and offers a reference to analyse mistakes.

One of the simplest ways you can use PuttView in practice is to project the ideal ball path for a selected putt. Then try to hit the ball down that line in order to test your ability to hit that line at the correct speed. By projecting the ball path, PuttView takes out the element of green-reading and provides you with distinct feedback on those two essential skills to putt well.

After hitting a few putts you can also analyse your shot pattern by comparing it to the ideal ball path. That way you can easily figure out if your mistake was in direction or speed.

From a coaching and learning perspective, the uses of PuttView are varied and numerous. We firmly believe that using PuttView can really change and improve the way golfers practice in the future because visualisation is such a key component of mastering the lost art of putting. Not only will you be able to see the line more clearly, you will be able to see the projected pace relative to that line which is vitally important. Once we have established that it is in fact possible for the ball to go in the hole and we know that in order to do so, it has to travel on the correct line at the appropriate pace for that line, hopefully we can start to form a visual image of just that. The ability to project an image onto the putting surface to help reinforce that visualisation is both incredibly useful and powerful. Remember what we said about creating what we see?

In the section on Attention, we talked about becoming an attention detective to establish where having your attention works best for you. Using the various tools within the PuttView software allows the golfer to experiment and provides instant and actionable feedback. By experimenting with the width of the line, focusing on the first three feet of the putt to determine start line, focusing on the last three feet to determine entry point or using the aiming point tool, you will be able to discover what works best for you.

Regardless of which of the various visuals you choose to practice with, or indeed create your own custom tools which is also possible, we know one thing for sure. You will definitely gain a clearer understanding of the importance of pace and have a whole lot of fun in the process. To see PuttView in action, visit **puttview.com**

OUR CONCLUSIONS

WE really hope you have enjoyed the journey with us. Our hope is that you will have considered a different way to go about changing your putting story. It would be tremendous if you now have a sense of possibility for the future as opposed to a resignation of inevitable decline.

No matter what age you are or how long you have been playing the game we see absolutely no reason whatsoever that the next 12 months can't be one of transformation for your game. As we said at the very beginning, our personal experience is when we see players having a breakthrough on the greens this can and often does spread to the rest of your game. When you change your concept of how to putt you may also find your concept of how to play changing for the better.

You begin to embrace the lost art of golf and putting as opposed to being lost in the science of technique.

You have the opportunity to change your story. Become the author of your own narrative as opposed to an actor just playing out a role given to you by someone else. Take charge of your script, be the one writing the sentences and paragraphs.

Engage in the process of taking ownership for your future experience of playing golf.

The joy of 'creating' putts can spread right across your game if not your whole life. What could you create? What could be possible?

With a real clarity of intent in the mind it is truly amazing what the body can achieve. We all tend to let our imagination muscle stagnate as we get older. Don't! So much happens in the imagination first, yet so few use it appropriately.

We also want to stress that this will not be a straight line of improvement. You will have some bad days on the greens. You will miss some short putts. That, we are afraid, is an inevitability of playing this game.

What isn't inevitable though is how you respond to those missed putts and poor rounds.

The way you react to what happens on the greens will be one of the key factors in how your story pans out.

If you react in the way you have always done then there is a very strong possibility of the story remaining the same. The problem with our reactions is that they are often laced with a high dose of emotion. Unfortunately (or fortunately, depending on how you react), the fact is that emotions are the glue of memory.

Emotion binds and holds us to a memory trace. For those of us past 21 years of age, we all remember where we were when those planes smashed into the twin towers on that dreadful September morning back in 2001.

This is a horribly apparent example in an extreme form of how emotion can be such a strong bind to an experience. Missing putts is trivial in comparison but the principle holds true. If we get emotional over the putts we miss then we are actually asking our brain to remember and repeat those experiences.

How did you react in the past to missing putts? Did you get lots of negative emotion rising in your system? What did you say to yourself?

For most people it is a story of emotion and confirmation.

Confirmation of the existing story: Here we go again. Just like me to three-putt again. Just another one of those days. Remember what we said early on in our time together.

What the thinker thinks the prover proves.

If I think I can't putt then my 'prover' is always looking for evidence to support that thought and there are more than ample opportunities to confirm my existing story.

We want you to close the pages of this book promising yourself to do something about your story.

Change your habitual responses and you will literally change the whole of your game.

A very simple technique we have used successfully over the years is what we call: Facts not opinions.

On the greens, we want you to deal in facts not opinions.

When you miss a putt and you call yourself an idiot, that is an opinion.

It may seem very apt at times – but it is an opinion.

When you say you just can't get the pace today, that is an opinion.

When you say it is going to be another one of those days, that is an opinion.

Can you see how all of these opinions we carelessly throw around and at ourselves have such a strong effect in confirming our existing negative and woeful putting story?

Thinker and prover, working hand in hand to keep you stuck in the mire of mediocrity.

Facts work differently. They are lanced of emotion as opposed to being laced with emotion. Get into the habit of factual responses: The putt was struck off the heel of the putter. It has gone long. I missed the pace on the low side. I mis-read it.

All of these facts give you something to do as opposed to something that just confirms an existing status quo.

Facts give you a direction, opinions keep you stuck.

Save your emotions for when you have created a putt exactly as you have seen it in your mind's eye. When you ask yourself good questions. When you give yourself a clear intent and when your body acts out that intention perfectly it is time to get emotional in the right way.

How wonderful is it that you created something in your mind that has come to pass in the physical world? You created the putt in your mind and made it real with your body!

It is vital when you do this that you reinforce this with emotion.

Engrave in your mind and body that feeling of creating a 20-foot, curling, right-to-left putt that just falls into the right edge of the hole at the perfect pace just in the way that you imagined it would.

When we get high on good putts your brain has a positive craving for more.

It says: "Repeat this again please. I want more of that."

It is the complete opposite of most golfers who show little-to-no emotion on holing a putt then allow themselves to erupt like a volcano when they miss what they perceive to be a putt that should have been holed.

We are unwittingly mixing the wrong emotional cocktail and perpetuating a story we don't like.

Resolve to change this from the moment you finish this book.

Commit to engaging yourself in the process of becoming great on the greens. Fall in love with the idea that you are developing a set of skills that can last and enhance the rest of your golfing life.

The ideas we have shared with you here are not just quick tips and drills lasting only as long as your attention drifts off onto the next 'secret' but a set of sound principles which can liberate your game and set you free to explore the outer edges of your capability.

Begin to create some wonderful putts as they can help you create some wonderful rounds and as you sit back reflecting on a round of golf with a smile on your face you will know the effort has been more than worthwhile.

All the very best,
Gary and Karl

• Karl and Gary host a number of Performance Putting Principles Schools and Masterclasses for individuals, groups and corporate clients at the stunning Archerfield Links on Scotland's Golf Coast.

To arrange a School or Masterclass, email gary@tpegs.com or karl@themindfactor.com.

Work with Gary

After spending 16 years traveling the world coaching over
30 European Tour pros, Gary set up TPEGS Ultimate Golf
Experiences with Sky Sports commentator and former Ryder Cup
player Andrew Coltart in 2011.
Based at Europe's premier Performance Centre at Archerfield
Links, TPEGS are now recognised as the go-to experts for One to
One Coaching, Master Classes, and Golf Events.

For further information visit **tpegs.com** and
archerfieldgolfclub.com or email gary@tpegs.com

Work with Karl

Karl has worked with golfers at all levels – including six major
winners – to help free up their game and release their true potential.
If you wish to explore the possibility of working on your own Mind
Factor with Karl on a one-to-one basis then structured personalised
programmes are available.
For overseas clients, there is a personalised one-to-one
Skype programme.
If you want to make a real difference with your students then
become a certified Mind Factor coach. Take your coaching to a
new level and join a growing community of coaches dedicated to
creating a lasting, lifelong, learning environment for their students.

For further information visit **themindfactor.com**

Watch tutorials from this book
Visit **nationalclubgolfer.com** and click on 'golf tips'